Katherine Bilsborough
Steve Bilsborough
Kirstie Grainger

Starlight

3
Student Book

W0044117

OXFORD
UNIVERSITY PRESS

Starter Back to School!

Vocabulary

1 **Discuss with a friend.**

1 How many people can you see?

2 What's the date today?

MONTHS

January
February
March
April
May
June
July
August
September
October
November
December

OCTOBER		
1st first	12th twelfth	23rd twenty-third
2nd second	13th thirteenth	24th twenty-fourth
3rd third	14th fourteenth	25th twenty-fifth
4th fourth	15th fifteenth	26th twenty-sixth
5th fifth	16th sixteenth	27th twenty-seventh
6th sixth	17th seventeenth	28th twenty-eighth
7th seventh	18th eighteenth	29th twenty-ninth
8th eighth	19th nineteenth	30th thirtieth
9th ninth	20th twentieth	31st thirty-first
10th tenth	21st twenty-first	
11th eleventh	22nd twenty-second	

How old are you?

1 I'm (eight) / nine.

What's your last name?

2 It's **Jones / Brown**!

When's your birthday?

3 It's on March **5th** / **10th**.

2 **Listen and circle the words. Listen again and repeat.** 🎧 01

3 **Listen, point and repeat.** 🎧 02

4 **Listen and circle the months. Listen again and chant along.** 🎧 03

Back to school and it's my birthday!
Hooray! Hooray! But when's your birthday?

(September) 1st, 2nd, 3rd?
November 4th, 5th, 6th?
December 7th, 8th, 9th?
10th, 11th or 12th?

Back to school …

September 13th, 14th, 15th?
November 16th, 17th, 18th?
December 19th, 20th, 21st?
30th or 31st?

Back to school …

5 Discuss with a friend.

1 Look at the picture. What objects can you see?

2 Which objects can you see in your classroom?

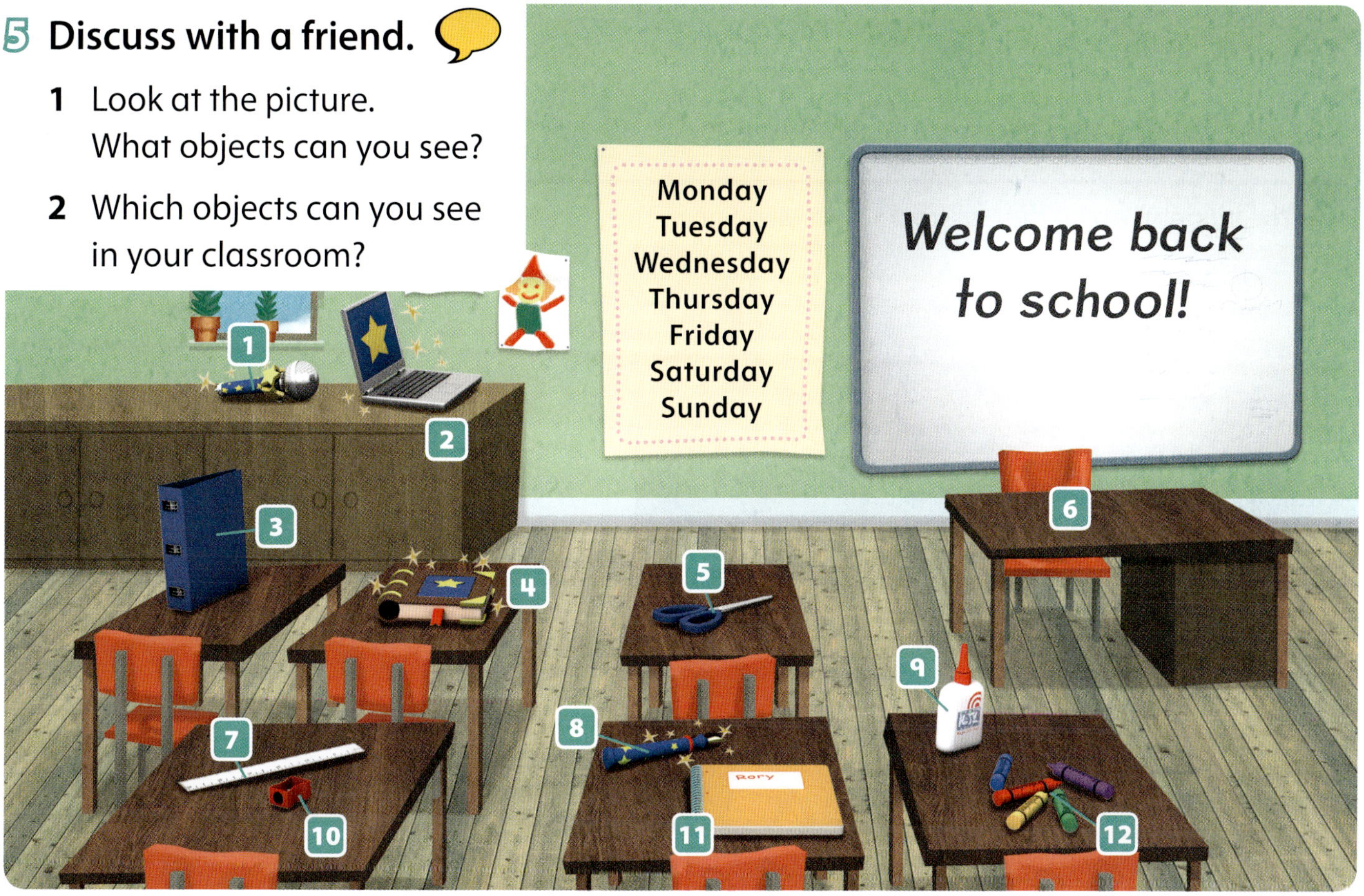

Monday
Tuesday
Wednesday
Thursday
Friday
Saturday
Sunday
Welcome back to school!
1
2
3
4
5
6
7
8
9
10
11
12
Rory

6 Listen and repeat. 04

7 Look and write the words. Listen again and check.

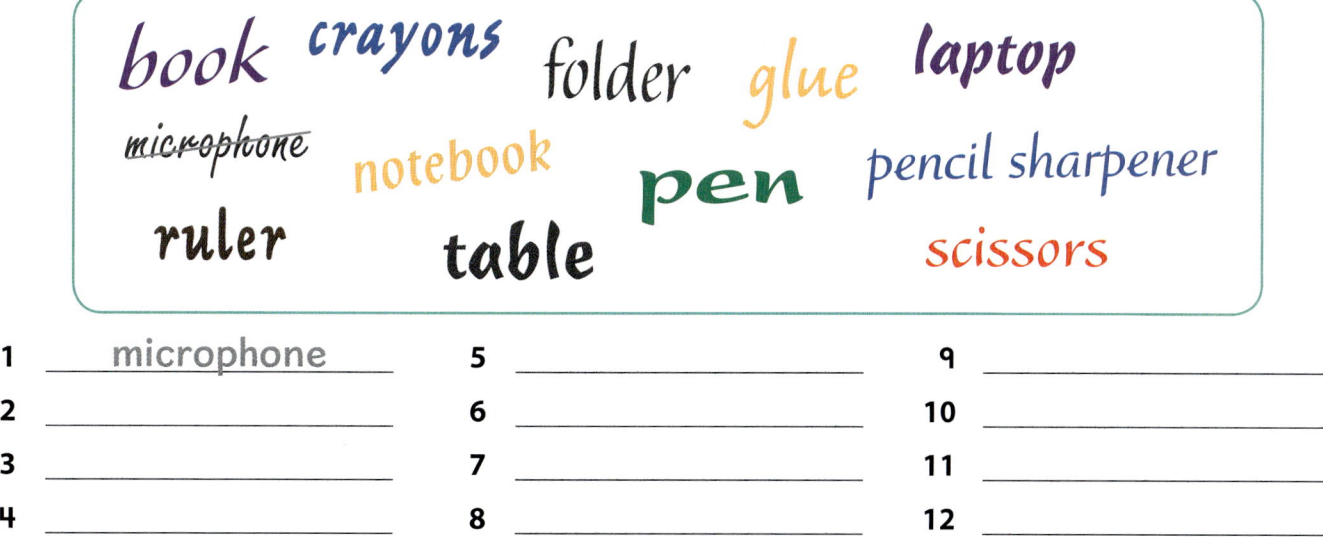

book crayons folder glue laptop ~~microphone~~ notebook pen pencil sharpener ruler table scissors

1	microphone	5		9	
2		6		10	
3		7		11	
4		8		12	

8 Say the words with a friend. Practice spelling the words.

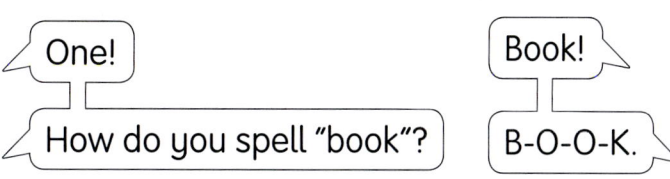

One!

How do you spell "book"?

Book!

B-O-O-K.

Miss Snow's Summer Show

1 Listen and read along.  05

1 The students are in the classroom with Miss Snow. They're very excited.

Good morning, everyone. This is a special lesson. It's a fun project!

There is a school show in the summer. You're a special team. You can help put on the show!

2 Miss Snow tells them about the show.

There are songs and stories in the show!

The show is on July 20th.

3 The students need special tools for the show.

Who would like this microphone?

Yes, please, Miss Snow!

This pen is for you, Rory.

4 There's a surprise for Rory and June. Their tools can do magic things.

Wow! Magic stories!

Wow! Magic songs!

5 Miss Snow gives Jeb a laptop.

Wow! Magic websites! I can find things out for the show.

6 Miss Snow has a very special tool for Rose.

This book is yours, Rose.

What can it do?

Let's see! Open it!

7 Rose opens the book.

Look at that!

Wow!

2 Act out the story.

1 Listen and say the colors.

2 Listen and say the dates.

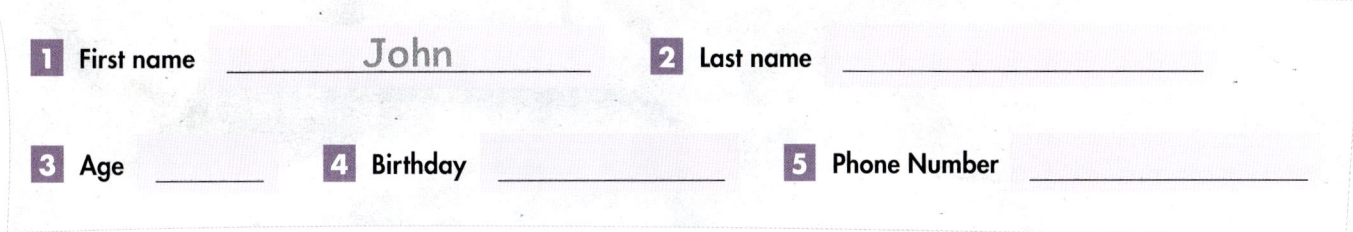

September 1st	September 2nd	September 3rd
September 4th	September 5th	September 6th	September 7th

3 Listen and write the information.

1 First name	John	**2** Last name	
3 Age		**4** Birthday	**5** Phone Number

4 Read and match the information. Listen and repeat.

1	First name		When's your birthday?		I'm nine.
2	Last name		What's your phone number?		It's on July 29th.
3	Age		What's your first name?		A-L-L-E-N.
4	Birthday		How old are you?		It's 450136.
5	Phone number		How do you spell your last name?		It's Sarah.

5 Draw the form in Activity 3.
Ask a friend the questions to complete the form.

How do you spell your last name?

When's your birthday?

A-L-L-E-N.

It's on July 29th.

1 Pop Stars

Vocabulary

1 Discuss with a friend.

1 What do the pop stars look like?

2 What does your friend look like?

2 Listen and repeat. 🎧 10

3 Look and write the words. Listen again and check.

| bangs   beard   braid   curly hair   earrings   eyebrows   freckles |
| glasses   mustache   ponytail   straight hair   wavy hair |

1 ponytail

2 _____

3 _____

4 _____

5 _____

6 _____

7 _____

8 _____

9 _____

10 _____

11 _____

12 _____

4 Play *Pick and Say* with a friend.

Number seven!   Glasses!

6

5 Look and read. Write *yes* or *no*.

1 The girl has curly hair.   yes

2 The woman has bangs.   _____

3 The children have glasses.   _____

4 Two people have curly hair.   _____

5 The man's beard is red.   _____

6 The man has a mustache.   _____

7 The girl has a braid.   _____

8 The woman has straight hair.   _____

6 Read and match the description with the picture. Listen and sing along. 🎵 11

He has wavy hair, big eyebrows, too
He doesn't have a mustache, oo oo oo!
She has a ponytail and freckles, too
She doesn't have earrings, oo oo oo!

They're the pop stars – yeah yeah!
They're the pop stars – yeah yeah yeah!

He has curly hair and bangs, too
And he has a beard, oo oo oo!
She has straight hair and glasses, too
She doesn't have a braid, oo oo oo!

They're the pop stars – yeah yeah!
They're the pop stars – yeah yeah yeah!

1    **2**    **3**    **4**

7 Look at the pictures in Activity 6 and play *Guess Who?* with a friend. 💬

He has wavy hair and big eyebrows.

Number 4!

Where's My Guitar?

1 Look at the pictures and discuss with a friend.

   1 What musical instruments can you see?   **2** Where do the children go?

2 Listen and read along. Write the names of the characters. 🎧 **12**

   Fred         

1 The Stars are famous pop stars. They have a big concert tonight, but Sam has a problem …

Are you ready, Sam? Let's play!

The STARS

Oh no! I don't have my guitar! Where is it?

2 Meanwhile, Pat, Molly and Fred are in the park. Pat and Molly are excited about the concert.

Look, Molly! The Stars have a concert tonight!

The STARS Concert Tonight!

They're my favorite pop group! I love Sam Star!

Who's Sam Star? Hmm … what's this?

3 Fred pulls and pulls and pulls. It's a guitar! Pat and Molly are excited.

Uff! Look! It says "Sam Star."

Sam Star

He doesn't have his guitar!

But he has a concert! Let's find him!

4 Pat, Molly and Fred go to the concert. But there are a lot of tall people. They can't see Sam Star.

THE STARS CONCERT TONIGHT

Where's Sam Star?

I don't know! I can't see. And we don't have tickets.

Sam needs his guitar. Fred, can you jump?

5 Fred can jump. He jumps up and looks for Sam.

Pat, who's Sam? *Does he have curly hair?*

No, he doesn't. He has straight hair.

6 Fred looks for Sam Star again. But there are still a lot of tall people.

Does he have glasses?

Yes, he does.

I can see him, but he's over there!

7 Fred has an idea. Molly, Pat and Fred crawl under the tall people.

Hey!

Excuse me, please!

They're tall, but we're short! Now we can see Sam.

8 Fred gives the guitar to Sam. Sam is very happy! Now the concert can start.

You have my guitar! Thank you! Here are tickets to the concert.

I love The Stars!

Me, too!

3 Act out the story.

1 **Look at page 9. Read and mark (✔) the answer.**

Does he have curly hair?

Yes, he does. ☐

No, he doesn't. ☐

Does he have glasses?

Yes, he does. ☐

No, he doesn't. ☐

2 **Look and answer the questions.**

Mike

Pat

Molly

Sophie

Sam

Fred

1 Does Molly have freckles? _No, she doesn't._____

2 Does Mike have a beard? _____

3 Does Sam have a mustache? _____

4 Does Pat have bangs? _____

5 Does Sophie have glasses? _____

3 **Listen and look at the pictures in Activity 2. Write the names.**  **13**

1 ___Fred____ 2 _____ 3 _____

4 Look at the pictures and complete the questions and answers.

1 Does the man _____have_____ glasses?   No, he doesn't.

2 _____ the girl _____ a braid?   No, she doesn't.

3 _____ the boy _____ ?   Yes, he does.

4 _____ the woman _____ ?   Yes, she does.

5 Unscramble the questions. Look at the pictures in Activity 4 and write the answers.

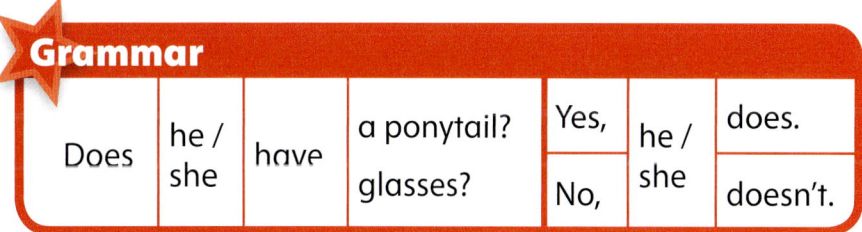

Grammar

Does	he / she	have	a ponytail? glasses?	Yes, No,	he / she	does. doesn't.

1 have / Does / bangs / ? / woman / the
   Does the woman have bangs?   _Yes, she does._

2 Does / straight hair / ? / boy / the / have
   _____   _____

3 the / have / Does / a / ponytail / ? / girl
   _____   _____

4 man / a / beard / ? / have / the / Does
   _____   _____

6 Look at the pictures in Activity 2 and play *Question Whiz.*

It's a boy.

Yes, he does.

Does he have glasses?

It's Sam!

1 Circle the words with a friend. Listen and check. 🎵 14

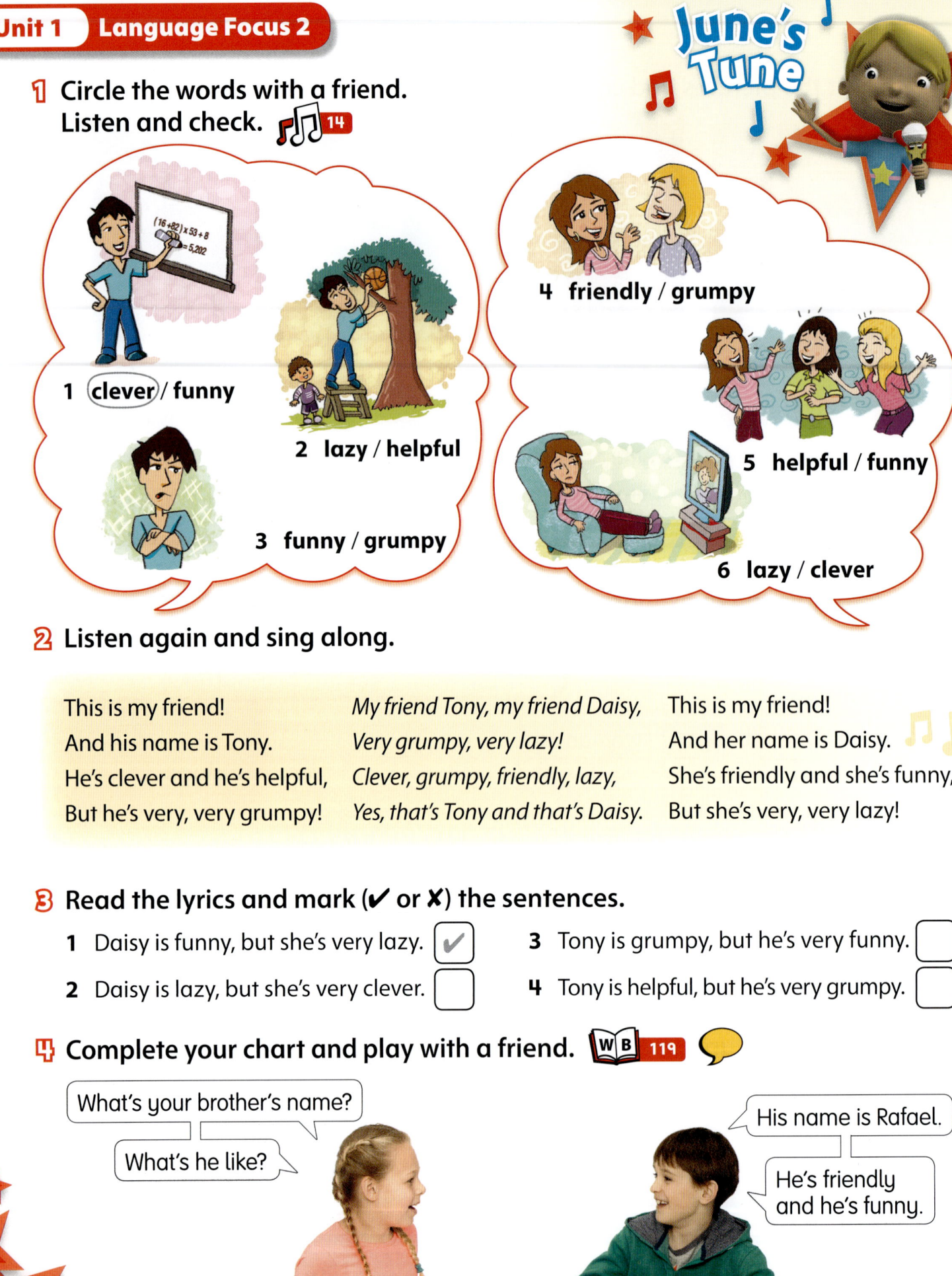

1 (clever) / funny

2 lazy / helpful

3 funny / grumpy

4 friendly / grumpy

5 helpful / funny

6 lazy / clever

2 Listen again and sing along.

This is my friend!	*My friend Tony, my friend Daisy,*	This is my friend!
And his name is Tony.	*Very grumpy, very lazy!*	And her name is Daisy.
He's clever and he's helpful,	*Clever, grumpy, friendly, lazy,*	She's friendly and she's funny,
But he's very, very grumpy!	*Yes, that's Tony and that's Daisy.*	But she's very, very lazy!

3 Read the lyrics and mark (✔ or ✗) the sentences.

1 Daisy is funny, but she's very lazy. ✔

2 Daisy is lazy, but she's very clever. ☐

3 Tony is grumpy, but he's very funny. ☐

4 Tony is helpful, but he's very grumpy. ☐

4 Complete your chart and play with a friend. WB 119

What's your brother's name?

What's he like?

His name is Rafael.

He's friendly and he's funny.

5 Read and mark (✔) the chart for Max and Lorna.

What's Max like?

He's friendly and he's funny. He's helpful, but he's lazy.

What's Lorna like?

She's funny, but she's grumpy. She's lazy, but she's very clever.

6 Look at the chart and complete the questions and answers.

1 What's Jane like?   She's ___friendly___ and she's _____.

2 _____ Charlie _____? He's _____, but _____.

3 _____ Max _____? _____ and _____.

4 _____ Lorna _____? _____.

Grammar

What's	Max	like?	He's	funny and	he's	helpful.
	your friend		She's	clever, but	she's	grumpy.

7 Write questions and answers about family members. Ask and answer with a friend. 📖 💬

What's your sister like?
She's clever, but she's grumpy.

What's your grandpa like?
He's funny and he's friendly.

13

1 Listen and read along. Match the description with the pictures. 🎧 15

Rose Knows about ...

Portraits

Artists paint *portraits* to show how people look. A portrait is a picture of a person or people. When we look at portraits, we can see the *appearance* of the person, their *expression* (are they happy or sad, for example), and the objects that are important to them.

1 She is sitting. She has a guitar and she is wearing a black dress and a hat. The background is brown.

2 She is standing next to a bucket. She is wearing a long white dress and a hat. In the background, we can see flowers and trees.

3 He is standing. He has a stick in his hand. He is wearing a gray sweater. In the background, we can see clouds in the sky.

4 He is sitting on a tree trunk. He is wearing a white shirt and brown shorts.

2 Read again and complete the chart.

	Expression	Appearance	Objects
1	happy	black dress	guitar
2			
3			
4			

3 Complete the *Information Card* with words from Activity 2.

"Boy with a Wheelbarrow"
1880 (oil on canvas)
by Ernst Josephson (1851–1906)

This is a portrait of a boy. He is (1) ___serious___.
He is (2) _____ in a garden. He is wearing
(3) _____ and he has (4) _____
hair. He has a wheelbarrow.

4 Draw a portrait of a friend and write an *Information Card*.

1 Listen and number the pictures.
Listen again and repeat. 🎧 16

2 Listen and repeat the sentences. 🎧 17

Silly Sally wears
socks in the sea and
sings on the sand.

Sunny Street

Strong Stan stands by the
street under the statue
and eats strawberries.

A Musical Instrument

Jeb's Value ...

Materials

★ Guitar: one empty cereal box, one paper towel roll, three rubber bands

★ Drum: one empty cylindrical oatmeal box with cover, two wooden spoons

★ Shaker: one empty plastic water bottle with lid, dried beans or lentils

★ Colored paper, colored acrylic paint, brush, glue, self-adhesive tape, sequins or confetti

★ **Read and stick.**

Be quiet and listen when other people are performing.

Stage 1: Plan your project.

1 Work in groups. Create a band. Think of a name.

2 Decide which instrument you want to play.

3 Collect the materials you need for your instrument.

Stage 2: Develop your project.

1 Make your instrument. Test it and decorate it.

2 Get together with your band. Experiment making sounds. Choose a song to play and practice.

Stage 3: Share your project.

1 Show your instruments to other bands.

2 Play your song to other bands.

3 Look at the audience: is everyone quiet and listening?

Stage 4: Evaluate your project.

Save your *Project Record*.

1 **Look and complete the questions and answers.**

 Mario  Lisa  Esther  Jerry  Jordan Ana

1 Does Mario have a beard?

_____ .

2 What's _____ like?

_____ and _____ .

3 Does _____ have freckles?

_____ .

4 What's _____ ?

_____ , but _____ .

5 Does _____ ?

Yes, he does.

6 What's _____ ?

_____ and _____ .

2 **Write your answers.**

What About You?

 Who's your favorite pop star?

_____

 Does your favorite pop star have long hair?

_____

 Does your favorite pop star have glasses?

_____

 Who's your favorite character in the story?

_____

 Does your favorite character have freckles?

_____

 What's your favorite character like?

_____

 What's your best friend like?

_____

 Does your best friend have curly hair?

_____

3 **Ask and answer the questions with a friend.**

Who's your favorite pop star?   Candy Hill!

Vocabulary

1 Discuss with a friend.

1 What sports are the children doing?

2 What sports do you like doing?

2 Listen and repeat. 🎧 18

3 Look and number the words. Listen again and check.

___ dancing	___ playing soccer	___ riding a horse	___ surfing
___ fishing	___ playing tennis	_1_ running	___ swimming
___ playing basketball	___ riding a bike	___ sailing	___ walking

4 Play *Look It Up* with a friend. 💬

Running!

Number one!

5 Complete the words.

1 s a <u>i</u> l <u>i</u> n g

7 wa __ k __ __ g

2 r __ d __ __ g
a   h o r __ __

8 p l __ __ __ n __
b a __ k __ t b __ l l

3 s w __ __ m __ __ g

9 f i __ __ i __ __

4 p l __ y __ __ g
t __ n __ i s

10 r __ d __ n __
a   b i __ e

5 __ __ a y __ n g
__ o __ c __ r

11 d a __ c __ n __

6 r u __ n __ __ __

12 s u r __ __ n __

6 Mark (✔) the sports the singer likes. Listen and sing along. 🎵 19

 ✔  ☐  ☐  ☐

It's Sports Day! Hooray, hooray!
It's Sports Day! Let's go and play!

Oh, I like sailing. I like fishing.
I like riding a horse!
I like playing basketball,
Riding a bike and walking, of course!

It's Sports Day! …

But I don't like running or surfing.
I don't like dancing at all!
I don't like playing soccer,
Playing tennis or swimming, at all!

It's Sports Day! …

I Don't Like Jumping!

1 **Look at the pictures and discuss with a friend.**

    1 How many frogs talk in the story?   **2** What sports can you name?

2 **Listen and read along. Write *true* or *false*.** 🎧 **20**

    1 Frank likes playing basketball. <u>true</u>   **3** Frank doesn't like swimming. _____

    2 Phil doesn't like surfing. _____   **4** Fiona and Phil like jumping. _____

1 Frank the frog is in the water with his friends. The other frogs are jumping. They like jumping. *Does Frank like jumping? No, he doesn't!*

2 Jumping is important for frogs. Fiona and Phil want to help Frank. Phil has an idea.

3 Phil and Frank stand on big leaves. Phil likes surfing. *Does Frank like surfing? Yes, he does!*

4 Phil surfs and Phil jumps. Frank surfs, but he doesn't jump.

5 Now Fiona has an idea. Frank likes swimming! Fiona jumps into the water and she swims. But Frank doesn't jump into the water.

Come on, jump! You like swimming!

I like swimming, but I don't like jumping. Sorry!

6 Suddenly, something hits Frank on the head. It's big and it's orange.

What's that?

It's a basketball.

Ouch!

7 The other frogs like playing basketball. *Does Frank like playing basketball? Yes, he does!*

Ooh! This is fun!

Look at Frank!

He's jumping!

Hey! Look, everyone! Frank's jumping!

8 Frank plays basketball with the other frogs. It's lots of fun.

Do you like playing basketball, Frank?

Yes, I do! I like surfing, swimming and playing basketball. And now I like jumping, too!

Yippee!

3 Act out the story.

1 Look at pages 20–21 and circle the answers.

1 Does Frank like jumping? Yes, he does. (No, he doesn't.)

2 Does Frank like surfing? Yes, he does. No, he doesn't.

3 Does Frank like playing basketball? Yes, he does. No, he doesn't.

2 Listen and complete the chart. 🎧 21

✔ = likes ✗ = doesn't like

Grammar

Does	he / she	like	dancing?	Yes,	he / she	does.
	Frank		surfing?	No,		doesn't.

	⛵	🏄	🎣	🏃	🎵	🥢
Frank	✗	✔	✔	✔	✗	✔
Phil	✗	✔	✗	✔	✔	✔
Felix		✔		✔	✗	✔
Fiona	✔	✔	✔			
Dora	✔	✗	✔	✗	✔	✔
Flo	✔				✗	✗

3 Look at the chart and write the answers.

1 Does Flo like sailing? Yes, she does.

2 Does Phil like fishing? _____

3 Does Dora like running? _____

4 Does Frank like walking? _____

4 Look at the information and complete the questions and answers.

Name: Anna

Likes:

Doesn't like:

Name: Billy

Likes:

Doesn't like:

1 Does Anna _____ like _____ swimming?   Yes, she does.

2 _____ Billy _____ riding a bike?   Yes, he does.

3 _____ like fishing?   No, she doesn't.

4 _____ Billy like _____ ?   No, he doesn't.

5 _____ surfing?   Yes, she does.

5 Write the questions and answers.

1   Does Billy like riding a bike?   Yes, he does.

2   _____   _____

3   _____   _____

4   _____   _____

6 Cover your book. Play *Memory* with a friend.

Does Billy like sailing?

No, he doesn't.

23

June's Tune

1 **Look and write the numbers. Listen and check.** 🎧 22

___ bouncing the ball   _1_ catching the ball

___ throwing the ball   ___ basket   ___ points

2 **Read and complete. Listen and check.** 🎵 23

| bouncing | ~~catching~~ | basket | points | throwing |

Here we are at the basketball game!
Here we are at the basketball game!
See them run, see them play.
Here we are at the basketball game!

Look at him! Frank's his name.
He's **(1)** _catching_ the ball!
What a game!
Look at Frank! Watch him play!
He's **(2)** _____ the ball!
He's great today!

Here we are at the basketball game …

Look at Frank! The **(3)** _____'s over there!
He's **(4)** _____ the ball up in the air!
Look at Frank! Watch him play!
He's scoring lots of **(5)** _____ today!

Here we are at the basketball game …

3 **Listen again and sing along.**

4 **Complete your picture and play with a friend.** WB 120 💬

What's number two doing?

He's throwing the ball.

5 Listen and draw lines.

Jane   Peter   Paul

Jim   Vicky   Lily

6 Look at the picture in Activity 5 and answer the questions.

1 What's Paul doing?   He's _____ riding _____ a bike.

2 What's Jane doing?   She's _____ a ball.

3 What's Jim doing?   _____.

4 What's Vicky doing?   _____.

5 What's Peter doing?   _____.

7 Draw a picture of five friends in the playground. Describe your picture to a friend. Point, ask and answer with a friend.

Peter is throwing a ball. Carla is running.

What's he doing?

He's throwing a ball.

Grammar

What's	Paul	doing?	He's	throwing a ball.
	Jane		She's	riding a horse.

25

1 **Listen and read along.
Number the pictures.** 🎧 25

Rose
Knows about ...

Safe
Sports

It is important to play sports safely. We can do a lot of activities before, during and after sports to protect our bodies and keep them safe.

1 When we exercise, our *heartbeat* and breathing are fast and we get hot. Soccer players wear shorts and T-shirts during a game to keep their bodies cool.

2 During a game, it is important to protect our bodies. Soccer players wear *shin pads* to protect their legs, and they wear soccer shoes to help them on grass.

3 Before and after sports, it is important to stretch to warm up our *muscles*.

4 Soccer players need to drink water before and after a game, because their bodies use lots of water when they play.

shin pads

muscles

stretches

1

2 **Read again and complete the chart.** 📝

Soccer Players ...	When?	Why?
drink water		
wear shorts and a T-shirt		
do stretches		
wear soccer shoes		
wear shin pads	During	To protect their legs

3 Complete the *Scrapbook Label* with words from Activity 2.

This is me at school. I'm **(1)** __playing soccer__. I'm wearing
(2) _____ to protect my **(3)** _____.
I'm also wearing **(4)** _____ to keep my body cool,
and **(5)** _____ because they are good for running
on grass.

4 Read and complete the *Scrapbook Label* with words from the box.

eyes   help him swim   swimming   ~~swimming pool~~

This is my brother, Max! He's in
the **(1)** __swimming pool__. He's
(2) _____. He's wearing goggles to
protect his **(3)** _____. He's also wearing
fins to **(4)** _____.

goggles

fins

5 Write a *Scrapbook Label* for a photo of yourself.

1 Listen and number the pictures.
Listen again and repeat. 🎧 26

2 Listen and repeat the sentences. 🎧 27

Chuck the chicken eats cheese and
chocolate under a chair!

Shirley the sheep wears shorts.
She wears a shirt and shoes as well!

27

Pulse Rate Charts

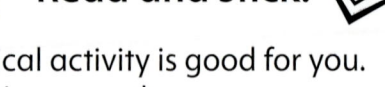

Jeb's Value ...

Materials

★ Classroom clock with second hand

★ One ruler per student

★ One pencil per student

★ One sheet of grid paper per student

★ **Read and stick.**

Physical activity is good for you. Exercise every day.

Stage 1: Plan your project.

1 Work with a friend. Think of two different activities to do and record them, for example:

   Slow exercise: walking in place for 2 minutes

   Fast exercise: jumping in place for 2 minutes

2 Use the pencil and ruler to make two charts for slow and fast exercise.

3 Practice measuring your pulse.

 ### Stage 2: Develop your project.

1 Take turns measuring your pulse at rest. Write down the number of beats per minute.

2 Take turns doing the slow exercise. Measure your pulse every minute.

3 Repeat with the fast exercise.

Stage 3: Share your project.

1 Attach your charts to a classroom wall.

2 Present your results to other teams.

3 Discuss with the class. Why is it important to exercise every day?

Stage 4: Evaluate your project. WB 26

Save your *Pulse Rate Charts*.

Slow Exercise	
Exercise Type	Walking
Exercise Times	Beats Per Minute
before	75
1 minute after	80
2 minutes after	86
3 minutes after	91

Fast Exercise	
Exercise Type	Jumping
Exercise Times	Beats Per minute
Before	75
1 minute after	83
2 minutes after	97
3 Minutes after	110

1 Look and complete the questions and answers.

1 Does he like swimming?

  No, he doesn't_____.

2 _____?

  Yes, _____.

3 Does _____?

  No, _____.

4 What's she doing?

  She's _____.

5 What's _____?

  _____.

6 _____?

  He's _____.

2 Write your answers.

What About You?

 1 Which sports do you like doing?

  _____

 2 Does your best friend like all these sports, too?

  _____

 3 What's your best friend doing now?

  _____

 4 Which sports don't you like doing?

  _____

 5 What do you do before sports?

  _____

 6 What do you do after sports?

  _____

3 Ask and answer the questions with a friend.

Which sports do you like doing?

I like dancing and I like playing basketball.

1 Play *Number Quiz.*

1 Does your mom/dad/brother/sister have …

      **?**

2 Does your mom/dad/brother/sister have …

      **?**

3 Does your mom/dad/brother/sister like …

      **?**

4 What's your friend like …

     **?**

5 What's he doing …

      **?**

6 What's she doing …

      **?**

My points: _____   My friend's points: _____

Australia

1 **Match the words with the pictures.**

| 2 | dancing | | wildlife | | surfing |

2 **Read and label the paragraphs.**

~~Sports~~   Animals   Traditions

Australia is in the continent Oceania. It is a big island. The capital city is Canberra. Most people in Australia speak English. Australia is famous for the outback, which is a very big and dry part of the country. Australians like spending time outdoors because of the sunny, warm climate and all the open space.

1

a _____Sports_____

Australians love going to the beach. Water sports, like swimming, sailing and surfing, are very popular. Australians also like other sports, for example: soccer, tennis and rugby.

2

b _____

Aboriginal Australians have a very long and interesting history. Aboriginal dances, like *Corroboree*, are part of their culture. People paint their faces and dance to traditional music.

3

c _____

Australia is famous for its wildlife. You can find a lot of animals there, like kangaroos and koalas.

 3 **Complete the Venn diagram with outdoor activities.**

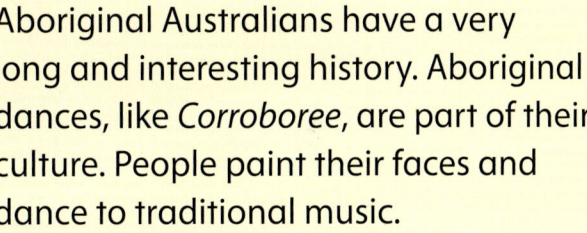

Australia   **Where I Live**

Both

tennis

Vocabulary

1 **Discuss with a friend.**

   1 What jobs can you name?

   2 What job does your mom or dad do?

Today!

2 **Listen and repeat.** 28

3 **Look and write the words. Listen again and check.**

> actor   artist   astronaut   bus driver   cook   doctor
> farmer   librarian   nurse   teacher   train driver   waiter

1 actor   **4** _____   **7** _____   **10** _____

2 _____   **5** _____   **8** _____   **11** _____

3 _____   **6** _____   **9** _____   **12** _____

4 **Play** *Two in a Row* **with a friend.**

Numbers one and nine!

Actor and cook!

5 Listen and order the pictures (1–4). Listen and sing along.  29

 `1`

Look at him! He's a farmer.
He's a waiter, she's a cook,
A teacher and a bus driver, too.
Come and have a look!

Everyone's here! Ready? Lift-off!
The astronaut's ready to go.
Five, four, three, two, one!
Let's go, let's go, let's go!

Look at her! She's an artist.
She's a librarian, he's an actor,
A doctor, a nurse, a train driver, too!
Come and see them all!

Everyone's here! Ready? Lift-off!
The astronaut's ready to go.
Five, four, three, two, one!
Let's go, let's go, let's go!

6 Listen and mark (✔) the box. 30

1 What job does Sally's dad do?

A  B ☐ C ☐

2 Who is Sally's mom?

A ☐ B ☐ C ☐

3 What job does Sally's aunt do?

A ☐ B ☐ C ☐

4 Where is Sally's uncle?

A ☐ B ☐ C ☐

7 Play *Mime and Guess* with a friend.

Are you an artist?

Are you a cook?

No, I'm not.

Yes, I am!

33

A Visit to Planet Zing!

1 Look at the pictures and discuss with a friend.

   1 How many characters can you see?   **2** What jobs can you name?

2 Read and circle the words. Listen and check. 🎧 31

1 Arnie is an astronaut. He's on a strange, dark planet. The computer in the rocket is broken.

Oh no!

Can he fix the rocket?

No, he can't. We can't **go** / **going** home!

2 Arnie is reading about the planet. The cat and the dog see a strange shadow. They're scared.

Hmmm. *Can the aliens on this planet speak English?*

What's that? Can Arnie see it?

No, he can't. He's **read** / **reading**.

3 The shadow is coming closer. The cat and the dog are very scared now, but Arnie isn't **listen** / **listening**.

Can Arnie hear it?

No, he can't.

Can the aliens use a computer?

4 The shadow is a spaceship. The driver is an alien.

Hello! Welcome to Planet Zing! What's the problem?

I can't **fix** / **fixing** our rocket.

Phew! He's not scary!

5 The alien **have** / **has** a white coat and a black bag.

6 Suddenly, they hear a loud noise. It **isn't** / **aren't** a spaceship. It's a space bus! It's the alien's friend. He's a bus driver.

7 But *can he fix rockets? Yes, he can!*

8 5, 4, 3, 2, 1 ... blast off! The rocket takes off. It can **fly** / **flying** fast.

3 **Act out the story.**

1 Look at pages 34–35. Read and match the pictures with the questions and answers.

a Can Arnie hear it? | No, he can't.

b Can they fly home now? | Yes, they can.

c Can he fix the rocket? | No, he can't.

d Can he help? | No, he can't.

2 Listen and number the pictures. 🎧 **32**

Planet Wow

Planet Flash

Hello!

1

Planet Ting

!@?«&*%+Δ#

Planet Zap

3 Read and write the answers.

1 On Planet Ting, can the aliens cook?   No, they can't.

2 On Planet Flash, can the aliens rollerblade?   _____

3 On Planet Zap, can the aliens dance?   _____

4 On Planet Wow, can the aliens paint?   _____

4 Read and complete the questions and answers.

1 Can he __rollerblade__ ?
Yes, he can.

2 Can the baby _____?
No, she can't.

3 _____ cook?
No, she can't.

4 _____ run?
Yes, they can.

Grammar

Can	he / she	swim?	Yes,	he	can.
	your brother	make		she	
	they	cakes	No,	they	can't.

5 Mark (✔ or ✘). What can you and a family member do?

✔ = can
✘ = can't

Me				
My _____				

6 Write three questions about your friend's family member.

1 _Can your cousin ride a bike?_   _No, she can't._

2 _____   _____

3 _____   _____

4 _____   _____

7 Ask your friend the questions in Activity 6 and write the answers.

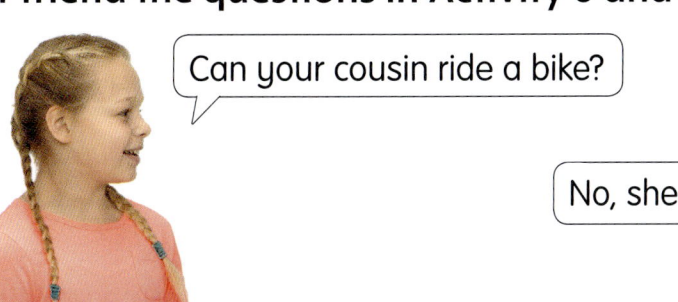

Can your cousin ride a bike?

No, she can't.

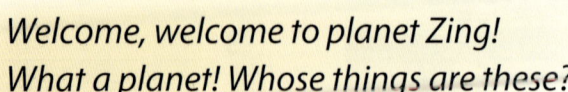

June's Tune

1 **Match the words with the objects. Listen and check.** 🎧 33

___ plasters   ___ blanket   _1_ medicine

___ cream   ___ bandage   ___ thermometer

Welcome, welcome to planet Zing!
What a planet! Whose things are these?

Look! It's the doctor's blanket,
And it's the doctor's cream.
It's the doctor's thermometer, too.
Hey! Doctor Zog! Yoo-hoo!

Welcome, welcome to planet Zing…

Look! It's the doctor's medicine,
And it's the doctor's plaster.
It's the doctor's bandage, too.
Oh, what a disaster!

Welcome to Planet Zing!

2 **Listen and sing along.** 🎵 34

3 **Look and complete the answers.**

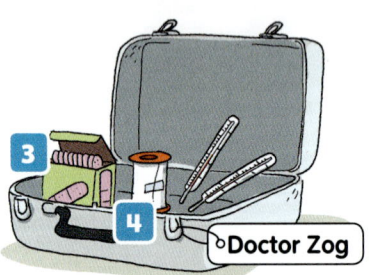

1 Whose medicine is this?
2 Whose blankets are these?
3 Whose plasters are these?
4 Whose bandage is this?

It's __Doctor Zig's medicine_____.
They're _____ blankets.
_____.
_____.

4 **Complete your picture and play with a friend.** WB 121 💬

Whose medicine is this?

It's Doctor Zig's medicine.

5 Look and complete the questions.

1 Whose books _are these_ ?
They're Ali's books.

2 _____ is this?
It's Sam's hat.

3 _____?
They're Ella's earrings.

4 _____?
It's Jen's bandage.

6 Look at the picture in Activity 5 again. Write questions and answers.

plaster   cream   ~~shoes~~   socks

1 Whose shoes are these?
They're Sam's shoes.

2 _____

3 _____

4 _____

Grammar

Whose	hat	is this?	It's	my	hat.
	earrings	are these?	They're	Ella's	earrings.

7 Draw pictures of objects that belong to family members.
Write questions and answers.

1 Whose computer is this? It's my brother's computer.

8 Ask and answer the questions with a friend.

Whose boots are these?

They're my mom's boots.

39

1 **Read and circle the words. Listen and check.** 🎧 35

Rose Knows about ...

Astronauts

What do astronauts (study) / carry / eat?

Astronauts travel to space in *rockets*. They study stars, planets and our solar system.

What do astronauts **read** / **wear** / **study**?

When astronauts go outside, they wear *spacesuits* to protect their bodies. They wear *helmets* with *sun visors* to protect their eyes.

rocket

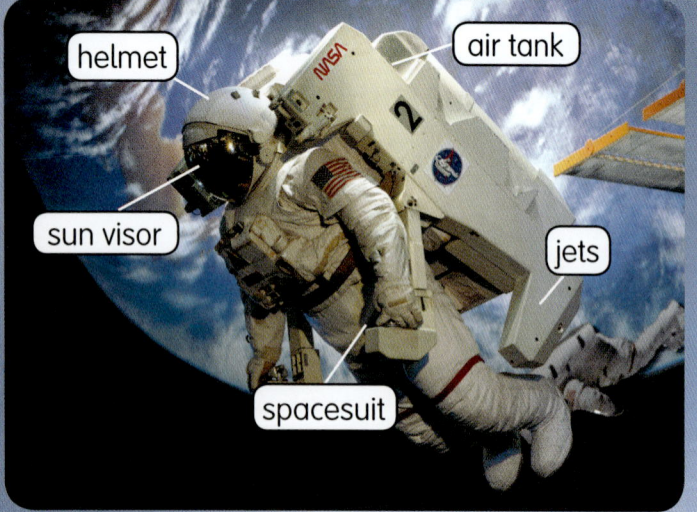

helmet

air tank

sun visor

jets

spacesuit

What do astronauts **carry** / **wear** / **eat**?

There is not any air in space. Astronauts carry *air tanks* so they can breathe. They have water tanks, too, so they can drink. They have microphones so they can talk to other astronauts, and cameras so they can take photos. Astronauts also carry *jets* or small rockets on their backs, so they can move in space.

2 **Read again and complete the mind map.**

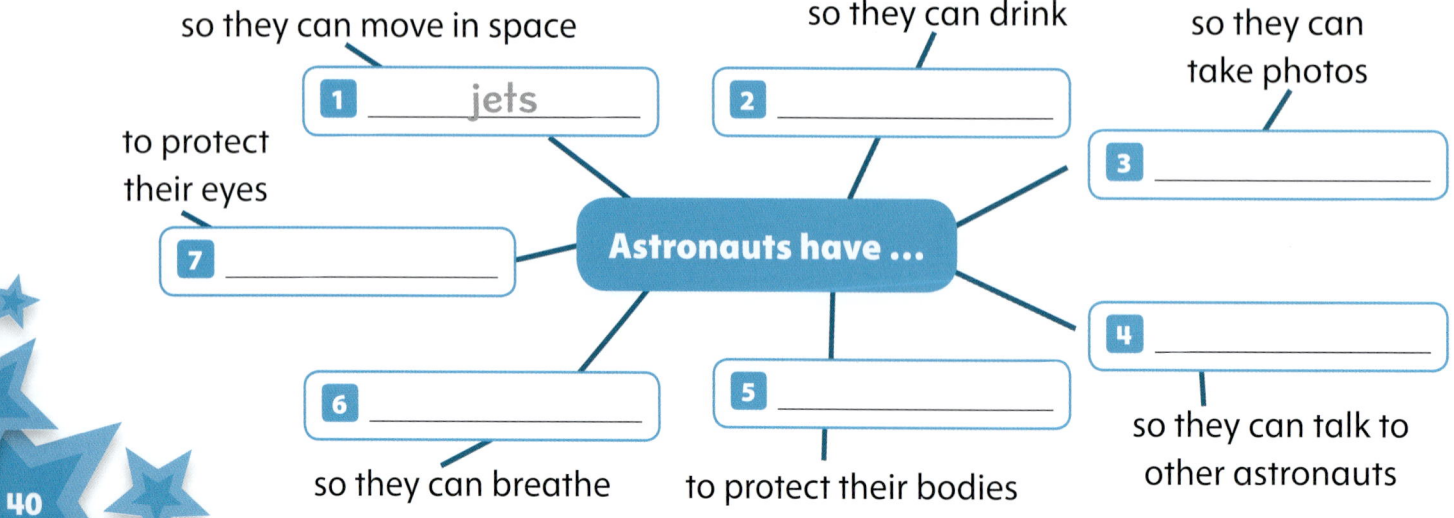

so they can move in space

so they can drink

so they can take photos

1 _____jets_____

2 _____

3 _____

to protect their eyes

Astronauts have ...

7 _____

4 _____

6 _____

5 _____

so they can breathe

to protect their bodies

so they can talk to other astronauts

3 Complete the *Spacesuit Advertisement* with words from Activity 2.

ARE YOU GOING TO SPACE?

**Come to SpaceGear for all your equipment!
At SpaceGear, you can buy:**

- <u>a spacesuit</u> to protect your _____<u>body</u>_____
- _____ to protect your _____
- _____ so you can _____
- _____ so you can _____

... and a lot more!

CALL 510 741064, OR GO TO SPACEGEAR.COM

4 Design and write a *Spacesuit Advertisement.*

Phonics

1 Listen and number the pictures.
Listen again and repeat. 🎧 36

2 Listen and repeat the sentences. 🎧 37

JULY

1

Seth takes a bath on the 5th of July and cleans his mouth and teeth.

The old lady has blond hair and eats food from around the world.

41

A New Uniform Poster

  Jeb's Value ...

Materials

★ One sheet of poster board

★ Ruler, pencil, scissors and glue stick

★ Pictures of uniforms from old magazines or the Internet

★ Colored pens and pencils

★ Read and stick.

Protect your clothes. Keep them neat.

Stage 1: Plan your project

1 Work in groups and discuss. Choose a job that needs a uniform.

2 Find pictures of people who do the job.

Stage 2: Develop your project.

1 Get together with your group and divide the poster board into two parts.

2 Cut out pictures of the people who do the job.

3 Make a collage with your pictures on the left. Then, design and draw a new uniform on the right.

Stage 3: Share your project.

1 Get together with your group. Attach your poster to a classroom wall.

2 Walk around the classroom and look at all the uniform designs.

3 Discuss with your group. Which uniforms are practical? How does each uniform look?

Stage 4: Evaluate your project.  38

Save your *Project Record*.

1 Look and complete the questions and answers.

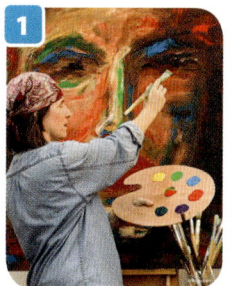    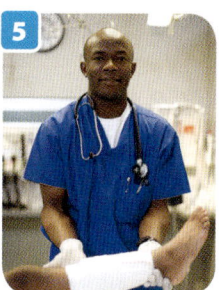 

1 Can <u>the artist paint</u> ?

Yes, <u>she can</u> .

2 _____ go to the Sun?

No, _____ .

3 _____ write?

_____ .

4 Whose medicine <u>is this</u> ?

It's <u>the nurse's medicine</u> .

5 Whose roller bandages _____ ?

They're _____ .

6 _____ books _____ ?

_____ .

2 Write your answers.

What About You?

 1 Think of a family member. What job does your family member do?

_____

 2 Can your family member speak English?

_____

 3 Can your family member rollerblade?

_____

 4 Can you play the piano?

_____

 5 Can you use a computer?

_____

 6 What's your dream job?

_____

3 Ask and answer the questions with a friend.

What job does your uncle do?

He's a teacher.

The Costumes Closet

1 Look at the pictures and discuss with a friend.

1 What jobs can you name?

2 What objects can you name?

2 Listen and read along. Complete the sentences.  38

1 It's _Miss Snow's wig_ .

2 It's _____ .

3 They're _____ .

4 They're _____ .

1 It's Saturday, July 20th. It's almost three fifteen. The students are in the school auditorium.

The costumes are in this closet.

Wow! They're great!

Do you like wearing a costume?

Yes, I do!

2 All the students like wearing costumes. Jeb is a cook. He's wearing a white hat.

Look at Jeb! He has a black mustache.

He has big, gray eyebrows, too.

He looks funny!

3 Now June is an astronaut, Rory is a farmer and Rose is a pop star.

What are you doing?

I'm riding a horse!

I'm walking on the moon.

I'm dancing!

4 Miss Snow likes wearing a costume, too. She's a nurse.

Look! I have a ponytail and a blue dress.

Miss Snow? Is that you?

5 Suddenly, a young student comes into the classroom.

6 The young students are playing soccer outside.

7 Miss Snow opens her bag.

8

3 Act out the story.

Vocabulary

1 Discuss with a friend. 💬

1 What animals can you name?

2 What is your favorite animal? Why?

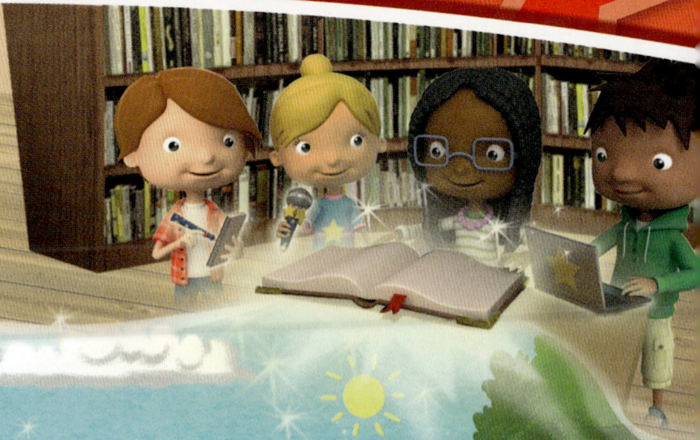

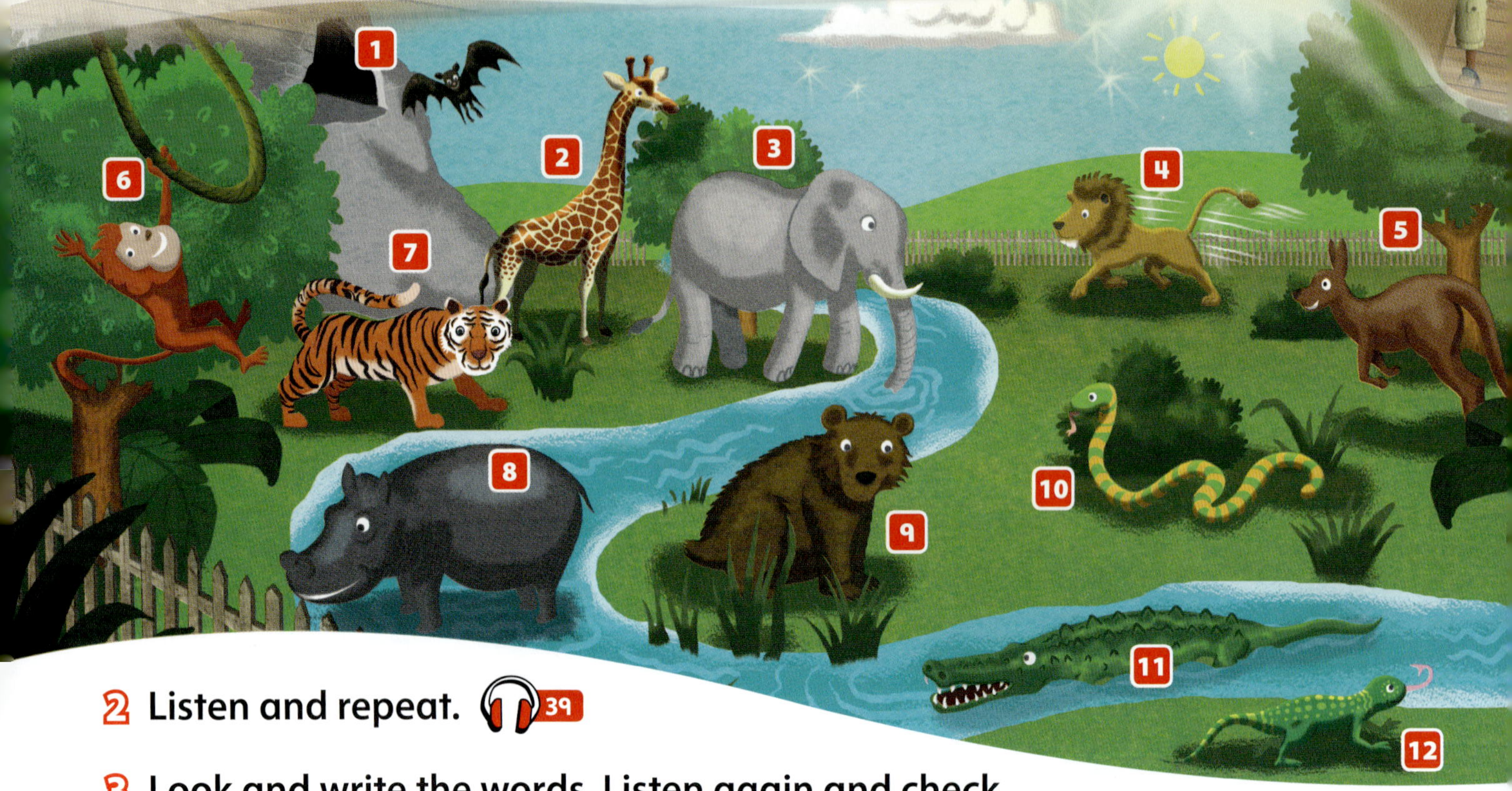

2 Listen and repeat. 🎧 39

3 Look and write the words. Listen again and check.

bat   bear   crocodile   elephant   giraffe   hippo
kangaroo   lion   lizard   monkey   snake   tiger

1 _____bat_____   4 _____   7 _____   10 _____

2 _____   5 _____   8 _____   11 _____

3 _____   6 _____   9 _____   12 _____

4 Play *Pick and Say* with a friend. 💬

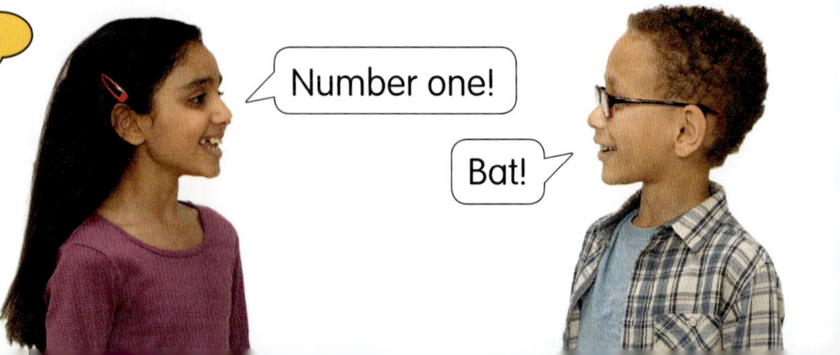

Number one!

Bat!

5 Look, read and complete.

 a bat
 a lion
 a kangaroo
 a snake

 a bear
 a lizard
 a monkey
 an elephant

1 This animal is big and gray.   an elephant

2 This animal has a long tail and it jumps very high. _____

3 This animal doesn't have legs and it is very long. _____

4 This animal lives in Africa and it has a mane. _____

5 This animal can fly, but it isn't a bird. _____

6 This animal likes bananas and swinging. _____

7 This animal is big and it is black. _____

8 The animal is green and it has a long tail. _____

6 Complete the words. Listen and check.  40

They're the animals in the zoo!
A b_e_ _a_r, a snake and a kangaroo,
An elephant, a tiger, a hippo, too!
They're the animals in the zoo!

The m___ nk___y is swinging.
The ___at is flying.
The l___ ___ ___rd is walking.
Ooh, ooh, ooh!
They're the animals in the zoo!

They're the animals in the zoo!
A bear, a snake and a kangaroo,
An elephant, a tiger, a hippo, too!
They're the animals in the zoo!

The c___ ___c___d___ ___e is swimming.
The ___ ___on is running.
The g___ raff ___ is eating.
Ooh, ooh, ooh!
They're the animals in the zoo!

7 Listen again and sing along.

What's a Kangaroo?

1 **Look at the pictures and discuss with a friend.**

1 What animals can you see?

2 What are the animals doing?

2 **Listen and read along. Number the animals as they appear in the story.** 🎧 41

 ☐    1    ☐    ☐

1 It's a sunny day in the safari park. The lion is looking for its friend. It sees the giraffe. The giraffe is new in the safari park.

Hello! Can you help me find my friend, the kangaroo?

Yes, of course!

What's a kangaroo?

2 The lion is short, but the giraffe is tall. It can see everything.

The grass is tall. I can't see!

I'm tall! I can see everything.

3 The lion and the giraffe look for the kangaroo. The giraffe sees an animal. It's flying around and around.

Ooh! Is this a kangaroo?

Is it jumping? Kangaroos jump.

Err … *No, it isn't.* It's flying.

Well, it isn't a kangaroo.

4 The giraffe sees another animal. It's in the water.

Look! A kangaroo!

Is it brown?

No, it isn't. It's green.

Well, it isn't a kangaroo. Kangaroos are brown.

5 The giraffe sees another animal. It's brown. It's swinging in the trees.

Are you a kangaroo?

No, I'm not. I'm a monkey.

Oh no! That's not a kangaroo!

6 The lion and the giraffe look for the kangaroo in the grass. The giraffe sees another animal.

Hello! Are you a kangaroo?

A kangaroo? Me? Of course I'm not a kangaroo!

Err … It isn't brown and it isn't jumping!

7 The lion and the giraffe look for the kangaroo next to the water. The giraffe sees another animal.

Look! A kangaroo!

Is it jumping?

Yes, it is! And it's brown.

Croak!

8 The giraffe runs after the frog. And the lion finds its friend, the kangaroo.

Kangaroo! Come back!

Hi!

But … here's the kangaroo! GIRAFFE! Here's the kangaroo!

3 Act out the story.

49

1 Look at pages 48–49. Match the questions and answers with the picture of the speaker.

Is it jumping?

No, it isn't.

Is it jumping?

Yes, it is!

2 Listen and number the pictures. 🎧 42

 1

Grammar

Is	it	eating?	Yes, it is.
	the giraffe	running?	No, it isn't.

3 Look at the pictures in Activity 2. Answer the questions.

1 Is the elephant eating?
   <u>No, it isn't.</u>

2 Is the lizard climbing?
   _____

3 Is the hippo sleeping?
   _____

4 Is the parrot drinking?
   _____

5 Is the giraffe eating?
   _____

6 Is the monkey swinging?
   _____

4 Write the questions.

1 (lion, sleep)   <u>Is the lion sleeping?</u>   Yes, it is.
2 (giraffe, drink) _____   No, it isn't.
3 (bat, walk)   _____   No, it isn't.
4 (kangaroo, jump) _____   Yes, it is.

5 Write questions and answers.

1 <u>Is she swimming?</u>   No, <u>she isn't.</u>

2 _____   Yes, _____

3 _____   No, _____

4 _____   Yes, _____

5 _____   Yes, _____

6 _____   No, _____

6 Look at the pictures in Activity 5 and play *Guess the Picture* with a friend.

Is it a boy or a girl?

Is he sleeping?

It's a boy.

Yes, he is.

June's Tune

1 Look and circle the habitats. Listen and check. 🎵 43

forest / cave

desert / forest

land / cave

water / jungle

jungle / water

cave / desert

2 Listen again and sing along.

Is your house a good place
for a kangaroo? No!
Is your house a good place
for a tiger, too? No!

Do tigers live in forests
And in jungles, too?
Do lizards live in deserts?
Yes, they do!

Is your house …
… for a hippo, too? No!

Do hippos live on land
And in water, too?
Do bats live in caves?
Yes, they do!

Is your house …
… for an elephant, too? No!

Do elephants like houses
With a kitchen and a hall?
No, they don't!
Not at all!

3 Read the lyrics and mark (✔) the answer.

			Yes, they do.		No, they don't.	
1	Do tigers live in caves?		Yes, they do.	☐	No, they don't.	✔
2	Do lizards live in deserts?		Yes, they do.	☐	No, they don't.	☐
3	Do hippos live on land and in water?		Yes, they do.	☐	No, they don't.	☐
4	Do bats live in water?		Yes, they do.	☐	No, they don't.	☐

4 Complete your chart and play.  WB 122 💬

Do crocodiles live in jungles?

Do they live in forests?

No, they don't.

No, they don't.

5 Match the animals with their habitats. Complete the questions and answers.

in water and on land   on land

1 Do snakes live _in water and on land_____? Yes, _they do____.
2 _____ in water and on land? No, _____.
3 _____? Yes, _____.
4 _____? No, _____.

6 Choose five animals. Write questions and answers.

bats   bears   crocodiles   elephants   giraffes   hippos
kangaroos   lions   lizards   snakes   tigers

1 Do kangaroos live in water?   No, they don't.

7 Play *Can you remember?* with a friend.

Do bats live in caves?   Yes, they do.

1 Listen and read along. Match the descriptions with the pictures. 🎧 44

Rose Knows about ...

Animal Habitats

The place where an animal lives is called its *habitat*. An animal is *native* to a place where its natural habitat is. Different habitats have different weather and food. Animals find the food they need in their habitats.

3 Some crocodiles are native to Africa. They need the sun and water, so they live in rivers and on land. They eat fish and small animals.

▢ Pandas need weather that is not too hot or too cold. They live in forests in China. They climb trees in the forest. Pandas eat *bamboo*.

▢ Polar bears need to live in the snow. They live in the Arctic, near the sea. It's very cold there and there's lots of snow. They swim in the sea to find food. Polar bears eat fish and *seals*.

▢ Kangaroos are native to Australia. They live in the long grass in hot places. Kangaroos eat grass and roots.

1

2

3

4

 2 Read again and complete the chart. 📝

Place	Animal	Weather	Food
Africa	crocodile		
		very cold	
			bamboo

3 Complete the *Animal Fact File* with words from Activities 1 and 2.

Animal Fact File	
Animal	
Color(s)	Black and white
Size	1.2 to 1.5 meters
Favorite weather	
Food	
Native to	
Another fact	They climb trees.

4 Draw your favorite animal. Write an *Animal Fact File*.

1 Listen and number the pictures.
Listen again and repeat. 🎧 45

2 Listen and repeat the sentences. 🎧 46

A young girl with a long earring is dancing, drinking and eating!

Stan the clown sees a man on the moon with a melon and a spoon.

55

Bird Feeding Station

Materials

★ One empty paper towel roll
★ One single-hole punch
★ Scissors
★ Two tongue depressors
★ Peanut butter
★ Birdseed
★ String

★ **Read and stick.**

Wild animals need a habitat. Protect the habitat of animals in your area.

Stage 1: Plan your project.

1 Decide where to place the bird feeder.
2 Copy the chart onto grid paper to record data.

Stage 2: Develop your project.

1 Punch two holes close to one end of the paper towel roll. Cut two slits along the tube. Slide a tongue depressor through each slit. Spread peanut butter on the tube. Then sprinkle the birdseeds on it. Pass the ends of the string through each hole and tie them.
2 Hang the feeder in the place you chose.
3 Look at the birds. Make a chart and write the number of birds that use the feeder.

Stage 3: Share your project.

1 Attach your chart to a wall.
2 Present your results to your classmates. Explain: How does your *Bird Feeding Station* help protect the habitat of animals in your area?

Stage 4: Evaluate your project.  50

Save your *Project Record*.

Day 1	Day 2	Day 3
12	17	22

1 **Look and write the missing questions and answers.**

1 _Is the bear swimming_ ?
No, it isn't.

2 Is the hippo sleeping?
_____ .

3 _____ ?
Yes, it is.

4 _Do kangaroos live on land_ ?
_____ .

5 _____ ?
Yes, they do.

6 _____ in forests?
_____ .

2 **Write your answers.**

What About You?

 Find a picture of an animal in this unit. Is it flying/swimming/running?
_____

 What are your favorite animals?
_____

 Do they live on land or in water?
_____

 What animals are native to your country?
_____

 Where do they live?
_____

3 **Ask and answer the questions with a friend.**

What are your favorite animals?

Lions, giraffes and tigers!

1 Play *Snakes and Ladders.*

	28 Is ... swinging?	27 Do ... in caves?	26 Whose is ...?	25 Can ... swim?
Finish				
20 Is ... sleeping?	21 Can ... climb?	22 Whose is ...?	23 Do ... in water?	24 Is ... jumping?
19 Do ... in water and on land?	18 Whose are ...?	17 Can ... run?	16 Is ... jumping?	15 Do ... in deserts?
10 Whose are ...?	11 Do ... in water?	12 Is ... walking?	13 Can ... jump?	14 Whose is ...?
9 Can ... run?	8 Is ... flying?	7 Do ... in caves?	6 Whose is ...?	5 Can ... fly?
Start	1 Can ... swing?	2 Whose are ...?	3 Do ... in jungles?	4 Is ... jumping?

Tanzania

1 Look at the pictures and choose the best title for the text.

A Visit to the Zoo   **A Wild Holiday**   **A Look at Tanzania**

2 Read and circle seven animals.

Tanzania is in East Africa. The capital city is Dodoma. Most people in Tanzania speak Swahili and English. One of the most famous places is Mount Kilimanjaro, which is the highest mountain in Africa, and is also a volcano.

The Serengeti National Park is the home of a lot of wild animals, like elephants, giraffes, lions, zebras and hippos. People can visit the Serengeti on *safaris* to see the wild animals in their natural habitats.

Tanzania is the home of many tribes. The Maasai are a famous tribe because of the respect and care they show for wild animals. The Maasai are *nomads*: they do not live in only one place. They move and live in different places. The Maasai have cows and goats. These animals are very important to them because they give the Maasai food and clothes.

3 Complete the chart with the names of wild animals.

Wild Animals	
Tanzania	Where I live
elephants	

Vocabulary

1 Discuss with a friend.

1 What foods do you eat at home?

2 What foods do you like?

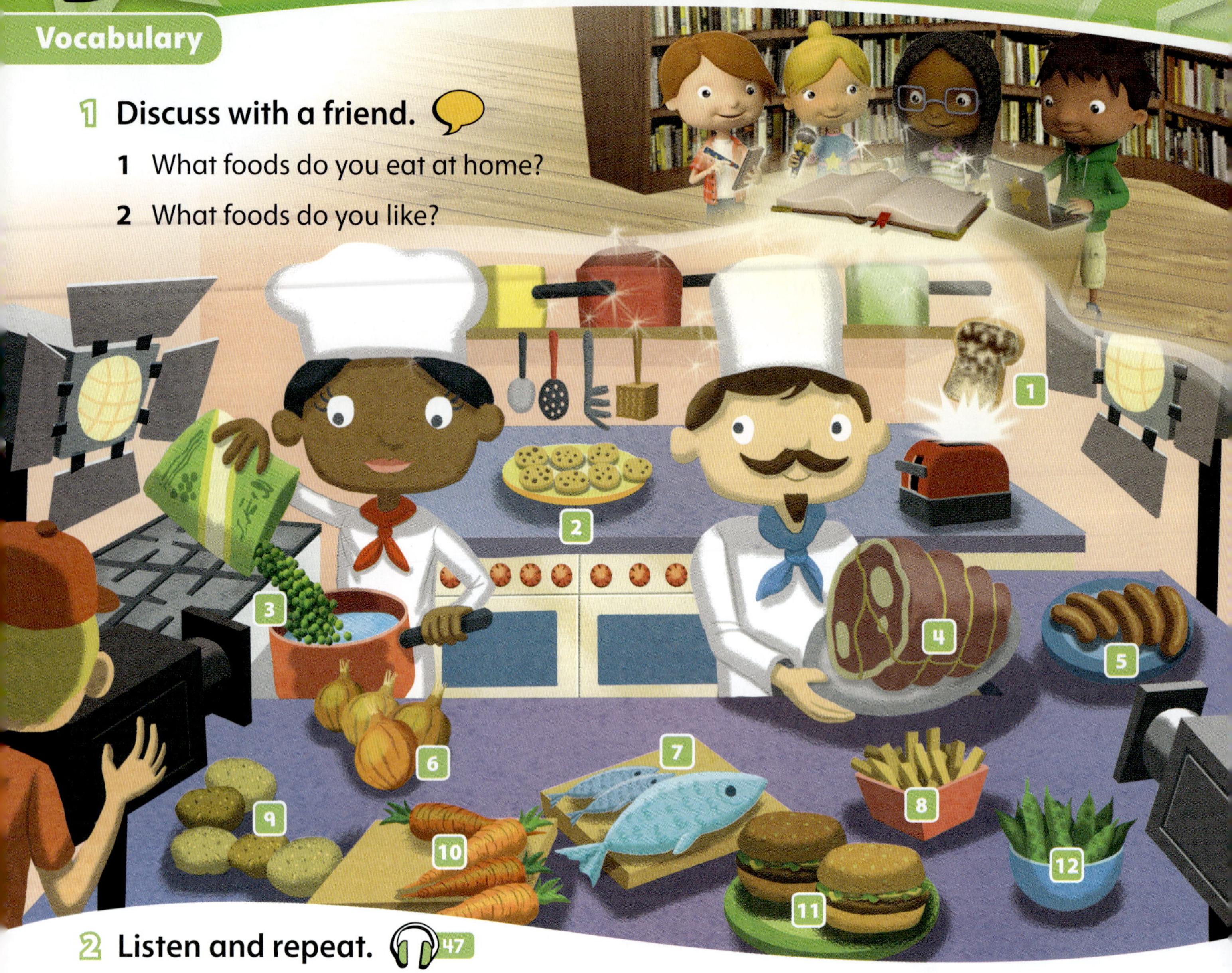

2 Listen and repeat. 🎧 47

3 Look and number the words. Listen again and check.

___ beans ___ cookies ___ meat ___ potatoes ___ burgers ___ fish

___ onions ___ sausages ___ carrots ___ French fries ___ peas _1_ toast

4 Play *Look It Up* with a friend.

Toast!

Number one!

5 Look and complete the descriptions.

1 _____Burger_____ and
_____ .

2 _____ ,
_____ and
_____ .

3 _____ ,
_____ and
_____ .

4 _____ and milk.

5 _____ and butter.

6 _____ and
_____ .

6 Listen and order the pictures (1–5). Listen again and sing along. 🎵 48

 1

Good morning! We're the cooks!
Here's our kitchen. Take a look!

We like fish and toast and meat.
Lots of lovely things to eat!

Good morning …

We like sausages, potatoes and peas.
Burgers with onions? Ooh! Yes, please!

Good morning …

We don't like French fries, cookies or beans.
We like carrots. Mmm! Yes, please!

7 Play *I like—I don't like* with a friend.

I like potatoes.   I don't like sausages.

Hungry Movie Stars!

1 **Look at the pictures and discuss with a friend.**

1 What foods can you name?   2 What jobs can you name?

2 **Read and complete the story. Listen and check.** 🎧 49

burger   fish   French fries   ~~lunchtime~~   sandwiches   sausages

1 It's __lunchtime__ on the movie set. Everyone is very hungry. Lunchtime is one hour.

I'm hungry.

Cut! It's lunchtime. Come back in one hour.

DIRECTOR

2 Tony, the cook, is cooking lunch for the actors, but the stars want special food. They aren't very friendly.

KITCHEN

Mmm, cheese _____.

Penelope, *would you like some cheese sandwiches?*

No, thank you! I'd like some chicken.

3 Lenny the waiter isn't very happy. He brings the stars chicken and _____.

Here you are.

We don't like this chicken.

We'd like some fish.

4 Lenny gives the chicken to the other actors. They're very happy.

Would you like some chicken?

Yes, please!

Hurry up!

5 Lenny brings the stars some fish, but they're very grumpy.

We don't like this _____.

I'd like a burger.

And *we'd like some sausages.*

6 Lenny brings the stars some sausages and a burger. He gives the fish to the other actors. Now they have a lot of food.

KITCHEN

Would you like some fish?

Yes, please! Thank you, Lenny!

Lenny, come here!

We don't like these _____ or the burger!

7 Lenny gives the sausages and the _____ to the other actors. Tony, the cook, is going home.

KITCHEN

Would you like a burger and some sausages?

Yes, please!

Where's Lenny?

We'd like some food!

8 It's two o'clock. It's time for work!

KITCHEN

CLOSED

Action!

Bye!

See you tomorrow, Tony!

Oh no!

Where's our lunch?

3 **Act out the story.**

1 **Look at pages 62–63. Circle the picture of the speaker.**

1   Penelope, would you like some cheese sandwiches? No, thank you!

2  Would you like some chicken? Yes, please!

3   I'd like a burger. And we'd like some sausages.

4   Would you like some fish? Yes, please!

2 **Listen and mark (✔) the chart.**  50

Ben		✔	✔		✔	
Lucy						
Kim						
Alex						

3 **Look and complete the sentences and questions.**

1  I'd __like some French fries__, please.

2  _____ like some _____, please.

3  __Would__ you like some _____? Yes, please.

4  Would you _____ some _____? No, thank you.

5  _____ some _____? Yes, please.

4 Complete the dialogue.

Waiter: Hello. _Would you like_ a burger?

Boy: No, thank you. _____ a sausage, please.

Waiter: _____ a potato, too?

Boy: No, _____. I'd _____ some salad, _____.

Waiter: Here you are.

Boy: Thank you!

Grammar

I'd like	a	burger.	Would you like	a	sausage?	Yes, please.
	some	carrots.		some	peas?	No, thank you.

5 Write your own dialogue. Use different food words.

Waiter: Hello. Would _____

You: _____

Waiter: _____

You: _____

Waiter: Here you are.

You: _____

6 Look at the chart in Activity 2. Play *Find the Person*.

Would you like a sausage?

Would you like some potatoes?

Are you Lucy?

Yes, please.

No, thank you.

June's Tune

1 **Write the words. Listen and check.** 🎵 51

afternoon breakfast dinner evening lunch ~~morning~~

1 in the ___morning___   **3** in the _____   **5** in the _____

2 have _____   **4** have _____   **6** have _____

Camera! Action! Work all day!
Camera! Action! Every day!
Camera! Action! Work all day!
Work all day then … cut!

It's breakfast time, breakfast time!
Orange juice and toast for me.
I have breakfast in the morning
Then I have a cup of tea.

Camera! Action! Work all day …

It's lunchtime. Lunchtime!
Chicken, chips and peas for me.
I have lunch in the afternoon
Then I have a cup of tea.

Camera! Action! Work all day …

It's dinnertime. Dinnertime!
Cheese, bread and salad for me.
I have dinner in the evening
Then I have a cup of tea.

Camera! Action! Work all day …

2 **Listen again and sing along.**

3 **Write the answers.**

1 When do you have breakfast?   I have breakfast in the morning.

2 When do you have lunch?   _____

3 When do you have dinner?   _____

4 Read and choose the answer.

1 **Mary:** When do you have lunch?

   Fred: A Yes, please.

   B Chicken and French fries.

   C In the afternoon.

2 **Mary:** What do you have for lunch?

   Fred: A In the afternoon.

   B I have sandwiches.

   C Yes, it is.

3 **Mary:** What do you have for dinner?

   Fred: A I have meat and potatoes.

   B Yes, please.

   C In the evening.

Grammar

When do you have	breakfast? lunch? dinner?	I have	breakfast lunch dinner	in the morning. in the afternoon. in the evening.
What do you have	for breakfast? for lunch? for dinner?	I have	toast and juice soup and salad chicken and potatoes	for breakfast. for lunch. for dinner.

5 Read the question and complete the answer.

On your birthday, what do you have for breakfast, lunch and dinner?

On my birthday, I have **(1)** _____ and **(2)** _____ for
breakfast. I have **(3)** _____ and **(4)** _____ for lunch.
(5) _____.

6 Complete your chart and play.  123

What do you have
for breakfast?

I have toast
and juice.

1 Read and color. Listen and check. 🎧 52

Rose Knows about ...

Healthy Eating

Our bodies need *nutrients* and *energy* to do activities and stay healthy. It is important to eat different foods to have a *balanced diet*. The *Eatwell Guide* is a picture that can help us decide what to eat from each *food group*. There are five food groups in the *Eatwell Guide*.

Oils and spreads

We only need a very small amount of oils, spreads, fats and sugars.

Dairy foods

We need dairy foods (milk, yogurt, cheese) for *protein* and *calcium*. We need calcium for strong bones and teeth.

Grains and tubers

Bread and pasta are made from *grains* (wheat, corn, rice). Potatoes and yucca are *tubers*: they grow in the ground. We need grains and tubers for *carbohydrates*. We need carbohydrates for energy.

Legumes and animal products

We need *legumes* (beans, lentils) and *animal products* (meat, fish, eggs) for protein. We need protein for strong muscles.

Fruit and vegetables

We need fruit and vegetables for *vitamins*. We need vitamins for a healthy body.

2 Read again and complete the chart.

Nutrients	Food Group	Why Do We Need These Nutrients?
Protein (P)	dairy foods, legumes and animal products	for strong muscles
Carbohydrates (CARB)		
Calcium (CAL)		
Vitamins (VIT)		

3 Complete the *Healthy Menu* with words from Activities 1 and 2.

THE HEALTHY CAFÉ

Appetizers
Tomato soup (VIT) with _bread (CARB)_

Chicken (P) and _____ (VIT)

Entrées
Rice (CARB), beans (P), cheese (_____),

tortillas (CARB) and salad (_____)

Desserts
_____ (_____) Banana smoothie:

and yogurt   bananas (VIT) and
(CAL + P)   _____ (CAL + P)

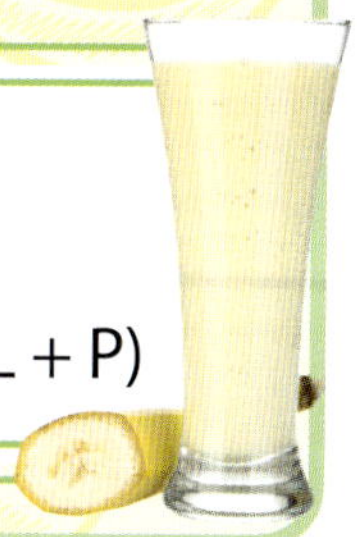

4 Create a *Healthy Menu*.

1 Listen and number the pictures. Listen again and repeat. 🎧 53

2 Listen and repeat the sentences. 🎧 54

Billy, the big pig, drinks milk with pink hippos!

Jean, the teacher, eats peas and ice cream on the beach next to the sea.

Food Pyramid

Jeb's Value...

Materials

★ One sheet of construction paper

★ Ruler, pencil, scissors and glue stick

★ Pictures of food from old magazines or the Internet

★ Colored pens and pencils

★ **Read and stick.**

Eat healthy foods to get the nutrients you need.

Stage 1: Plan your Project.

1 Work in groups. Make a list of the different types of food we eat.

2 Decide if we should have a small amount or a lot of the different foods.

3 Put the amount of food we should eat in order, from a little amount to the most.

Stage 2: Develop your Project.

1 Draw a food pyramid on the sheet of construction paper.

2 Cut out pictures of the different foods from old magazines or the Internet.

3 Glue the pictures onto the food pyramid. Put the foods we should eat only a little at the top and the foods we should eat the most at the bottom. Label the food groups.

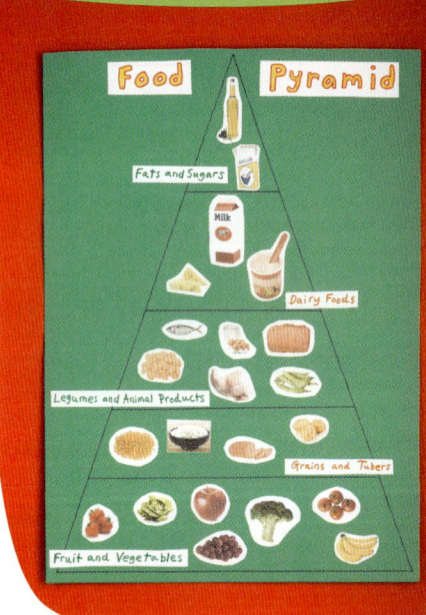

Stage 3: Share your project.

1 Get together with your group. Attach your food pyramid to a classroom wall.

2 Walk around the classroom and look at all the food pyramids.

3 Compare and contrast the results of another group with yours.

4 Discuss with your group. How much of the different foods do you eat? Do you get the nutrients you need every day?

Stage 4: Evaluate your project.  WB 62

Save your *Project Record*.

1 **Look and write the missing questions and answers.**

1 Would you _like some meat and_
_carrots_____?
_Yes, please_____.

2 _____
_____?
No, thank you.

3 When _____ lunch?
I have _____ in the
_____ .

4 When _____
_____?
_____ morning.

5 What _____ for dinner?
_____ for
_____ .

6 Would _____
_____?
Yes, _____ .

2 **Write your answers.**

What About You?

 1 What food do you like?
_____

 2 What food don't you like?
_____

 3 What do you have for breakfast?
_____

 4 What nutrients are in your breakfast?
_____

 5 Why do we need these nutrients?
_____

 6 What do you have for lunch?
_____

 7 When do you have dinner?
_____

 8 Would you like some fish for breakfast?
_____

3 **Ask and answer the questions with a friend.**

What food do you like? | I like chicken and carrots.

6 Superheroes

1 Discuss with a friend.

1 What activities do you do in the afternoon?

2 What activities do you do on the weekend?

2 Listen and repeat. 🎧 55

3 Look and number the words. Listen again and check.

___ brush my teeth	___ get dressed	___ go to bed	___ take a shower
___ do my homework	___ get up	___ go to school	_1_ wake up
___ feed the fish	___ go home	___ go to sleep	___ wash the dishes

4 Play *Two in a Row* with a friend.

Numbers one and seven!

Wake up and go to school!

5 Read the lyrics and circle the activities the superhero does after school. Listen and sing along. 🎵 56

Monday, Tuesday, Wednesday, Thursday
It's a Superhero Day!
Friday, Saturday and Sunday
It's a Superhero Day!

I wake up, I get up, I have a shower.
Wow! I'm a fast superhero today!
I get dressed, I brush my teeth, I feed the fish.
Wow! I'm a fast superhero today!

Monday, Tuesday, Wednesday, Thursday …

I go to school, I go home, I do my homework.
Wow! I'm a fast superhero today!
I wash the dishes, I go to bed, I go to sleep.
Phew! I'm a tired superhero today!

6 Complete the crosswords. Find the mystery activities.

1 | g | o | t | o | b | e | d |

 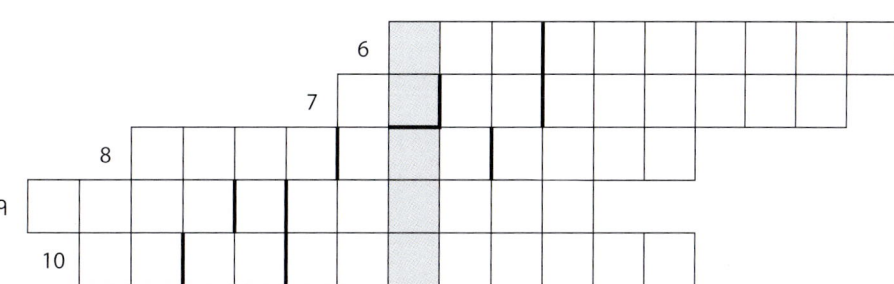 

The mystery activities are __g__ __ __ __ __ and __ __ __ __ __ __e__.

Superhero Schoolgirl

1 Look at the pictures and discuss with a friend.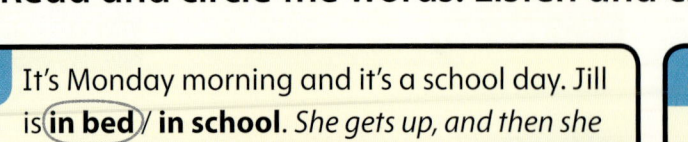

1 What daily activities can you name?

2 What pets does Jill have?

2 Read and circle the words. Listen and check. 🎧 57

1 It's Monday morning and it's a school day. Jill is **in bed** / **in school**. *She gets up, and then she takes a shower.*

Jill! It's time to wake up!

Yes, Mom!

I like Mondays!

2 *Jill gets dressed, and then she gets dressed again.* Why? Because she's a superhero!

Now I'm Ace Girl the superhero …

Now I'm Jill the **astronaut** / **schoolgirl**!

3 Jill can do special things with her superpowers. *She has breakfast* and *she feeds the fish* … at the same time!

Can you feed the **dog** / **fish**, please, Jill?

OK, Mom! No problem!

CEREAL

4 Then *she goes to school. She helps people* on her way.

Can you help me, please? My cat is under the **car** / **sofa**.

Wow! Thank you, Ace Girl!

Look! It's Ace Girl!

5 At recess, *she helps her friends* in the school playground.

Can you help me, please? My **kite / ball** is on the roof.

Wow! Look! It's Ace Girl!

She can fly!

6 Then *she goes home. She helps people on her way.*

Where's my **bag / key**? Can you help me, please?

It's under the seat!

Thank you, Ace Girl. You're fantastic!

7 At home, *Jill does her homework.* She's very tired. Superheroes work a lot!

Jill, can you help me, please?

Oh! I'm very tired.

OK! I'm coming. Don't worry!

8 But sometimes she doesn't need her superpowers!

Can you help me wash the **dishes / windows**, please?

Oh!

Of course I can, Mom!

3 **Act out the story.**

75

1 Look at pages 74–75. Complete the sentences in the story with 1, 2 or 3 words.

1 Jill ____likes____ Mondays.

2 She gets up, and then she __takes a shower__ .

3 She gets dressed, and then she _____ again, because she's a superhero.

4 She _____ and she has her breakfast at the same time.

5 She _____ her friends at recess.

6 She does her _____ at home.

7 She washes _____ for her mom.

2 Listen and number. Listen again and check.

3 Look at the pictures and complete the sentences.

On Monday evenings, Jill (1) _gets dressed_ , then she (2) _____.
She (3) _____ and she (4) _____ , and then she
(5) _____ .

4 Follow and complete the sentences.

On Saturday afternoons …

Sam

On Tuesday mornings …

Tim

On Wednesday evenings …

Mike

On Saturday afternoons, Sam **(1)** _does his homework_ . He has lunch, then he **(2)** _____ . He **(3)** _____ , and then he **(4)** _____ .

On Tuesday mornings, Tim **(5)** _____
_____ .

On Wednesday evenings, Mike **(6)** _____
_____ .

Grammar

He	wakes up,	then		goes to school.
She	gets dressed,		he	has breakfast.
Mike	takes a shower,	and then	she	feeds the fish.

5 Play *Who's this?* with a friend.

He plays soccer, and then he takes a shower.

That's right! My turn.

It's Sam.

June's Tune

1 **Write the times with a friend. Listen and check.** 59

> one o'clock   ~~seven fifteen~~   six fifteen
> ten thirty   three forty-five

seven fifteen _____ _____ _____ _____

2 **Listen again and sing along.**

Ace Girl, Ace Girl
Superhero schoolgirl!
What time do you wake up?

Every day, I wake up at seven fifteen,
Then I fly to school.
I have lunch at one o'clock.
Wow, Ace Girl, you're really cool!

Ace Girl, Ace Girl
Superhero schoolgirl!
What time do you fly home? (Repeat)

I fly home at three forty-five,
Then I have dinner at six fifteen.
I go to bed at night at ten thirty.
Wow, Ace Girl! That's a cool routine!

3 **Read and match the questions with the answers. Complete the answers.**

1 What time does Ace Girl fly home?

2 What time does she have lunch?

3 What time does she go to bed?

4 What time does she have dinner?

a She has lunch _____ at one o'clock.

b _____ at six fifteen.

c _____ ten thirty.

d _____ three forty-five.

4 **Complete your chart and play.** W B 124

What time does Ace Girl get dressed?

She gets dressed at seven thirty.

5 Complete the chart for yourself and a family member. Draw and write the times.

Me	___ : ___	___ : ___	___ : ___	___ : ___
My _____	___ : ___	___ : ___	___ : ___	___ : ___

6 Complete the questions and answers. Write the times.

1 What time do you __wake up_____? I wake up at _____.

2 What time does your _____ wake up? _____ wakes up at _____.

3 _____ you have breakfast?   I _____ at _____.

4 _____ your _____ have breakfast? _____ at _____.

Grammar

What time	do	you	have lunch?	I	have lunch	at	one eight five	o'clock. fifteen. thirty. forty-five.
	does	he / she your mom	go to bed?	He / She My mom	goes to bed			

7 Use the information in Activity 5 to play *Spy Interrogation* with a friend.

What time do you have breakfast?

I have breakfast at eight o'clock.

What time does your sister brush her teeth?

She brushes her teeth at eight o'clock.

1 Listen and read along.
   Circle the city names. 🎧 60

Rose
Knows about ...

Time Zones

Planet Earth is round. The sun only lights one part of the planet at a time.
When it is day in one country, it is night on the other side of the planet. The world has twenty-four different *time zones*. The time in places to the west of London is earlier, and the time in places to the east is later. The time in New York is five hours earlier than London. When it is 5:00 in the afternoon in the UK, it is *noon* in New York. When it is *midnight* in the UK, it is 7:00 in the evening in New York. It is important to know what time zone you are in when you travel to another part of the world or when you chat with friends that live in another country.

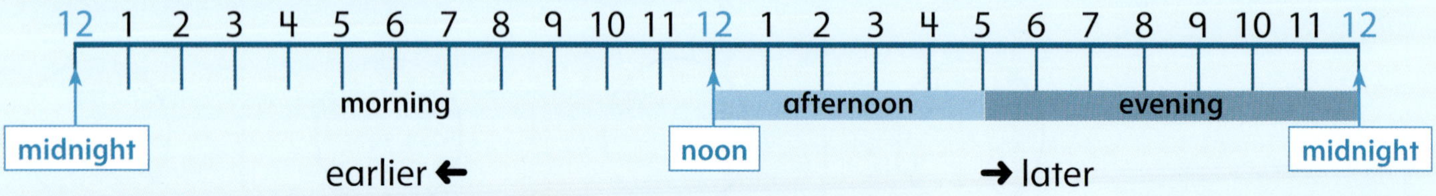

12 1 2 3 4 5 6 7 8 9 10 11 12 1 2 3 4 5 6 7 8 9 10 11 12

morning   afternoon   evening

midnight   noon   midnight

earlier ←   → later

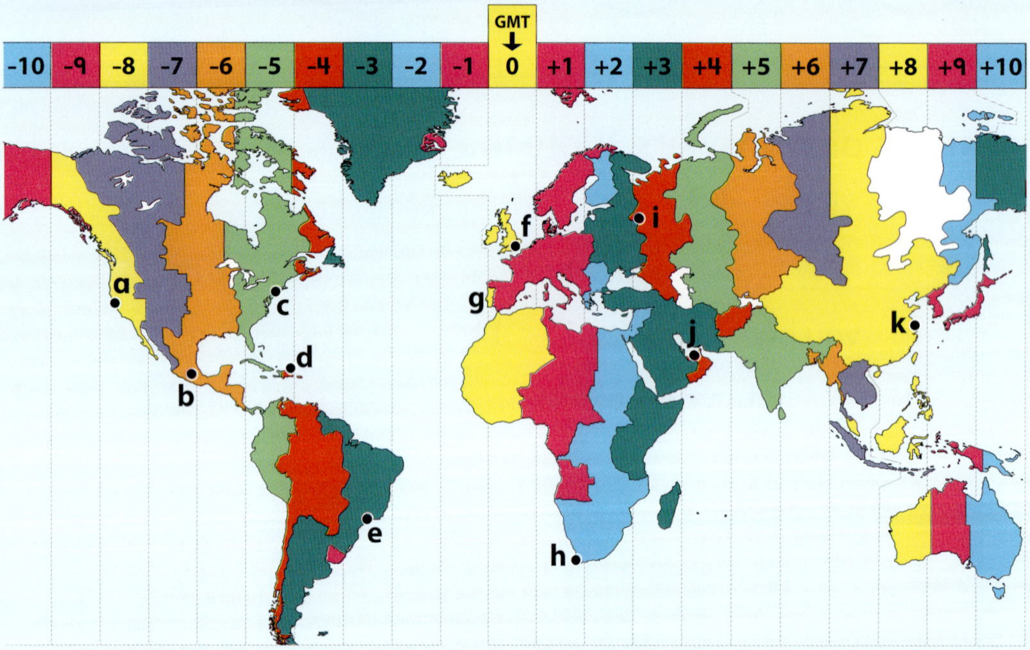

GMT
↓
-10 -9 -8 -7 -6 -5 -4 -3 -2 -1 0 +1 +2 +3 +4 +5 +6 +7 +8 +9 +10

a San Francisco
b Mexico City
c New York
d Puerto Rico
e São Paulo
f London
g Madrid
h Cape Town
i Moscow
j Abu Dhabi
k Shanghai

 2 Complete the chart with information from Activity 1.

City	Hour(s) Earlier or Later than London	Time When It's Noon in the UK	Time When It's Midnight in the UK
Shanghai	8 hours later	8:00 in the evening	
São Paulo			
Madrid			

3 Complete the *Web Chat* with words from Activities 1 and 2.

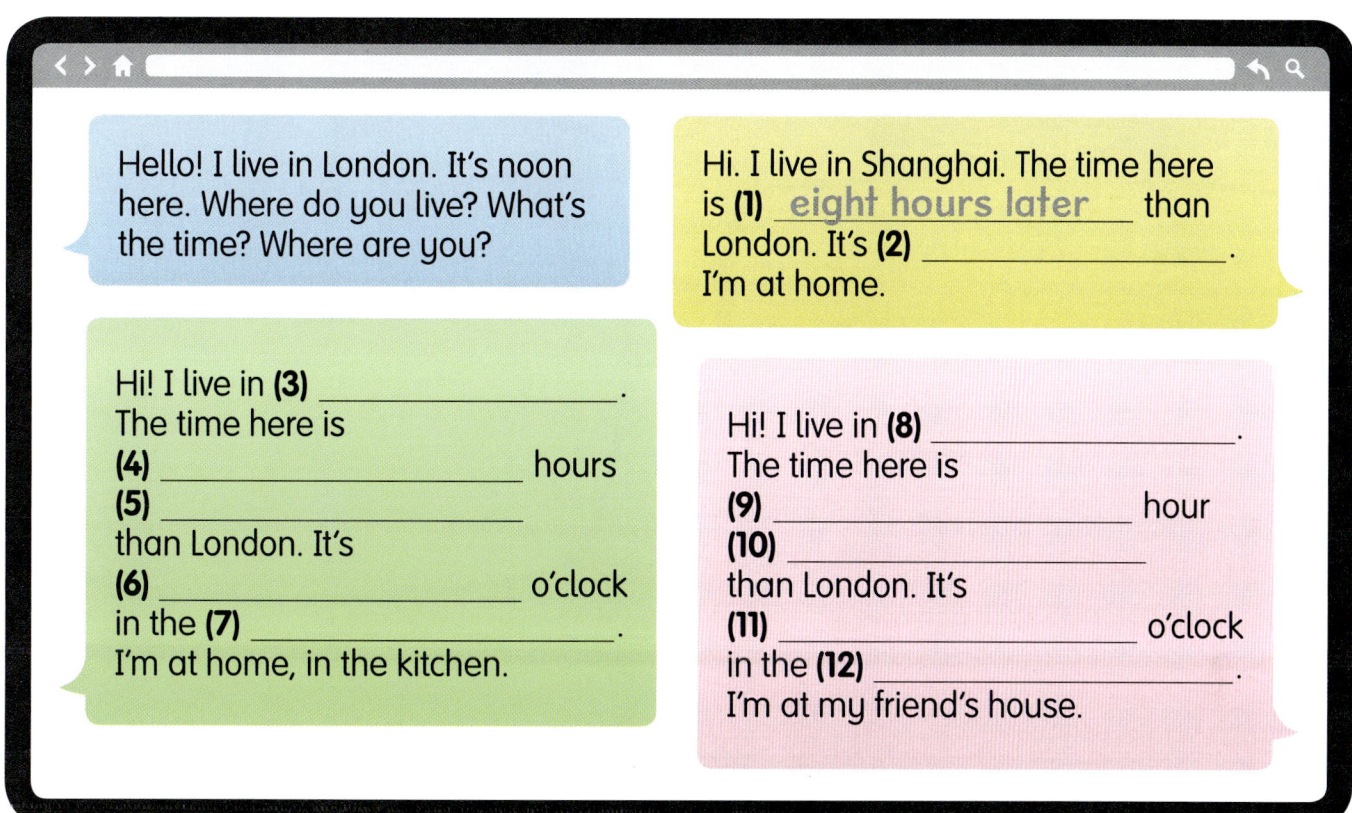

Hello! I live in London. It's noon here. Where do you live? What's the time? Where are you?

Hi. I live in Shanghai. The time here is **(1)** _eight hours later_ than London. It's **(2)** _____. I'm at home.

Hi! I live in **(3)** _____. The time here is
(4) _____ hours
(5) _____
than London. It's
(6) _____ o'clock
in the **(7)** _____.
I'm at home, in the kitchen.

Hi! I live in **(8)** _____.
The time here is
(9) _____ hour
(10) _____
than London. It's
(11) _____ o'clock
in the **(12)** _____.
I'm at my friend's house.

4 Choose different cities and write a *Web Chat* with a friend.

Phonics

1 Listen and number the pictures. Listen again and repeat. 🎧61

2 Listen and repeat the sentences. 🎧62

Oliver, the crocodile's friend, is a frog. He hops around a clock in orange socks!

Roland the robot is alone at home, sitting on the sofa, talking on the phone.

Daily Activities Chart

Jeb's Value ...

Materials

★ Grid paper

★ Ruler

★ Colored pens or pencils

 Read and stick.

Complete your assignments on time.

Stage 1: Plan your project.

1 Think of activities that you do. Choose a color for each activity. Make a key, for example: reading: blue; doing homework: red; watching TV: yellow.

2 Write how much time you spend every week doing each activity. Write the times.

3 Draw a chart for your activities. Write the days of the week and the number of hours.

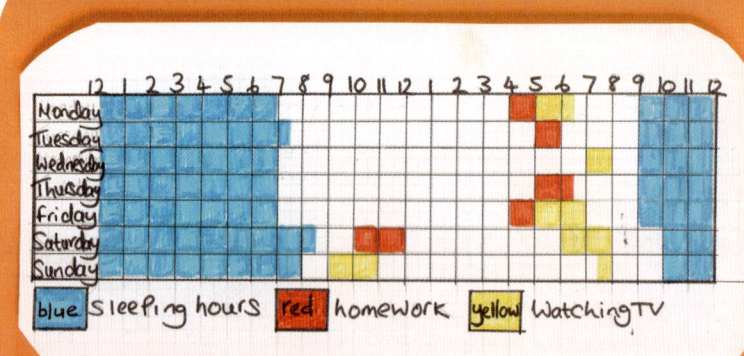

Stage 2: Develop your project.

1 Every day for one week, color in the squares for how long you spend on each activity.

2 At the end of the week, count the squares. Write the total number of hours for each activity.

Stage 3: Share your project.

1 Work in groups. Look at each other's charts.

2 Compare and contrast the results of your charts.

3 Discuss with your group: Do you spend enough time doing your assignments? Is there an activity that you can spend less time doing?

Stage 4: Evaluate your project. 74

Save your *Daily Activities Chart*.

1 Look and complete the sentences.

1 He has breakfast, and then

　　he brushes his teeth　　　　.

2 _____ goes

to school.

3 He goes home _____

_____.

4 She washes the dishes

　　at six fifteen　　　　　　　　.

5 _____

_____.

6 _____

_____.

2 Write your answers.

What About You?

 1 What time do you wake up?

_____

 2 What do you do in the morning?

_____

 3 What time do you have lunch?

_____

 4 What does your friend do
in the afternoon?

_____

 5 What time do you have dinner?

_____

 6 What do you do after dinner?

_____

 7 What time do you go to bed?

_____

 8 When it's noon in the UK, what time
is it where you live?

_____

3 Ask and answer the questions with a friend.

What time do you wake up?　　I wake up at seven o'clock.

1 Play *Four in a Row*.

Thailand

1 Look at the pictures and mark (✔) the place you want to visit. Tell a friend why.

2 Read and answer the questions.

1 What do Thai people love doing?

2 What animal do Thai people love?

Thailand is in Asia. There are a lot of languages in Thailand, but most people speak Thai. The capital city is Bangkok. There are more than eighty *canals* in Bangkok and many *floating markets*. From May to September, it rains almost every day. Thailand is famous for its delicious food, interesting temples and beautiful beaches.

Most Thai people love sharing their food with family and friends. They like eating rice, curry, soup, meat, fish and vegetables.

Thailand has thousands of temples. Some of the temples are very old. People often visit the temples on the weekend and on important days. A lot of the temples have statues of elephants. Thai people love elephants. They are a *symbol* of Thailand.

 3 Complete the Venn diagram with the names of foods.

Thailand   **Where I Live**

Both

rice

85

Who Needs Magic?

1 **Look at the pictures and discuss with a friend.**

    1 What are the students doing?   **2** What classroom objects can you name?

2 **Listen and read along. Write and draw the times.**

    1 The students are in the school auditorium at _ten thirty_.

    2 The school lunch is at _____.

    3 The show ends at _____.

    4 Miss Snow has some food for the students at _____.

1 It's Tuesday. It's ten thirty. The students are in the school auditorium.

We need to paint the scenery for the show.

And we need to make a website and a poster.

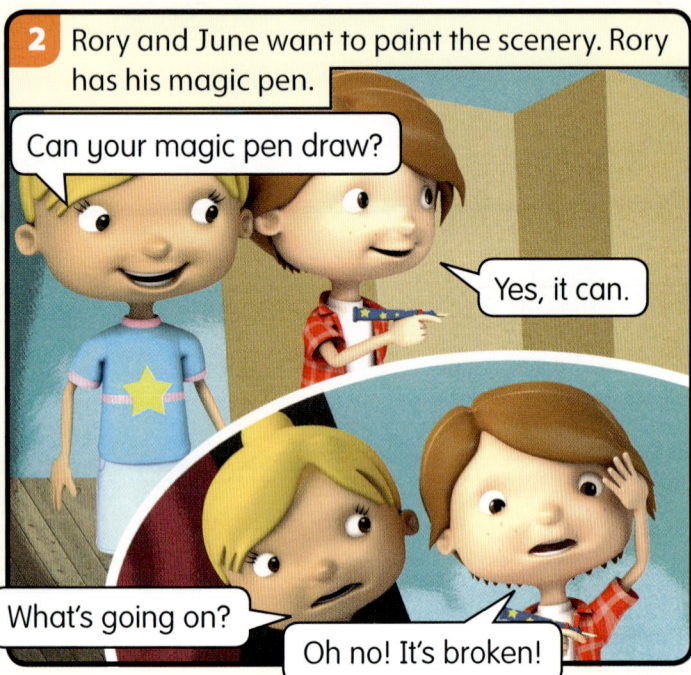

2 Rory and June want to paint the scenery. Rory has his magic pen.

Can your magic pen draw?

Yes, it can.

What's going on?

Oh no! It's broken!

3 Meanwhile, Jeb and Rose want to make a website and a poster.

Open your magic laptop, Jeb.

OK. Let's see.

What's going on?

Oh no! It's broken!

4 Now it's ten forty-five. School lunch is at twelve forty-five. They only have two hours.

Here's Miss Snow!

Hello, everyone!

Miss Snow, we can't draw the scenery. Our magic tools are broken!

We can't make the website or the poster.

5 Miss Snow has pencils and paint for Rory and June. She has crayons, scissors, glue and a laptop for Jeb and Rose.

6 Rory and June paint the scenery. They like painting.

7 Jeb makes a website and Rose makes a poster.

8 Now it's three o'clock! School lunch is over! But Miss Snow has hamburgers, French fries and fruit for the students.

3 Act out the story.

7 Fun Transportation Day

Vocabulary

1 Discuss with a friend.

1 What types of transportation can you name?

2 What types of transportation do you do use?

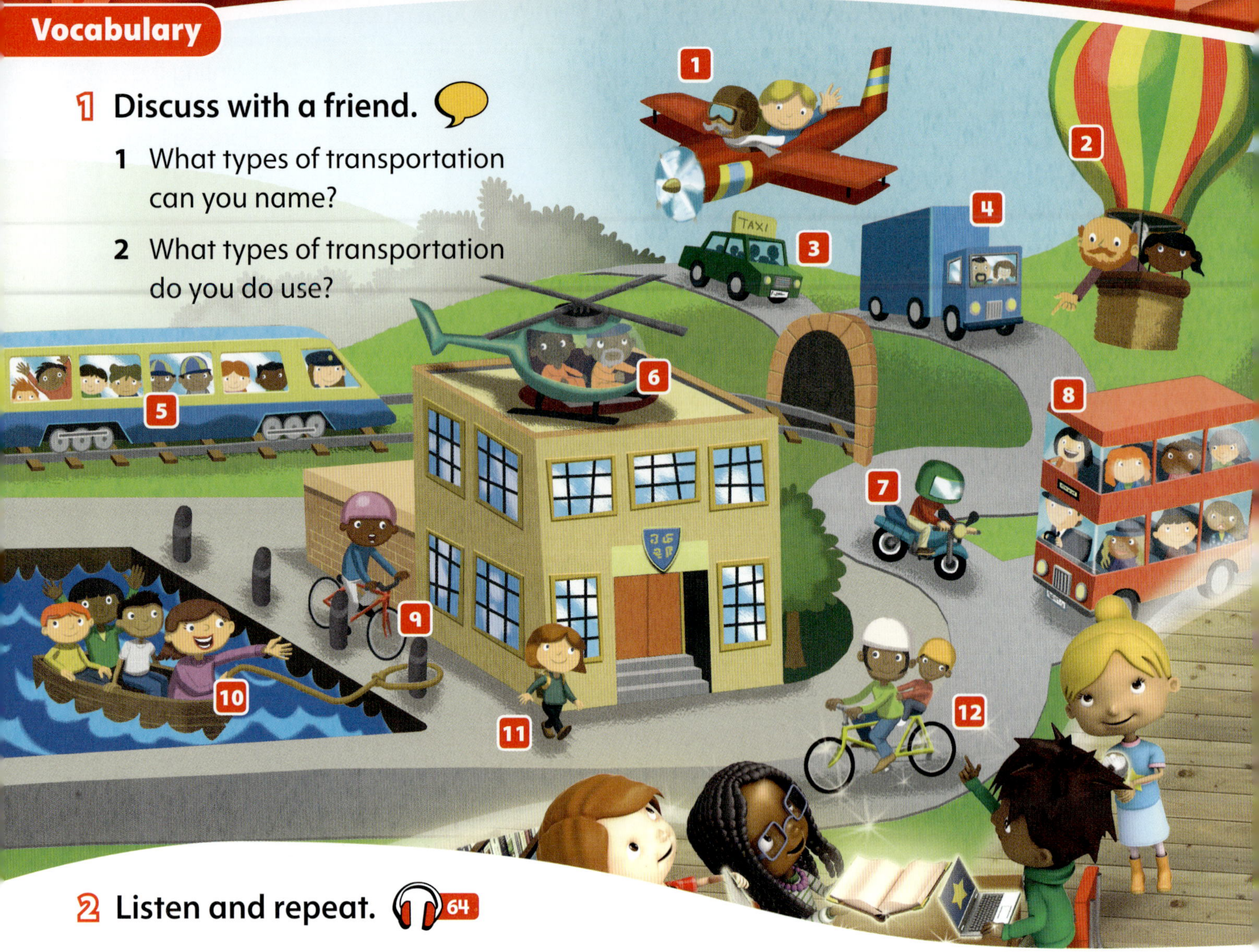

2 Listen and repeat. 64

3 Look and write the words. Listen again and check.

bike	boat	bus	helicopter	hot-air balloon	motorcycle
on foot	~~plane~~	tandem	taxi	train	truck

1 plane
2 ______
3 ______
4 ______
5 ______
6 ______
7 ______
8 ______
9 ______
10 ______
11 ______
12 ______

4 Play *Pick and Say* with a friend.

Number six!

Helicopter!

 **5** **Listen, color and draw.** 🎧 **65**

6 **Complete the words. Listen and check.** 🎵 **66**

I go to school on fo_ o _ t _ .
I go to school by ___ ___ke,
But I'd like to travel by lorry or bus,
Taxi or motorbike!

I'd like to travel by ___ ___at.
I'd like to travel by t___ ___ in.
I'd like to travel by
he___ ___c___ ___ ___er
To school and home again!

I go to school on foot…

I'd like to travel by tan___ ___m.
I'd like to travel by p___ ___ ___e.
I'd like to travel by ___ ___ t-___ ___r
b ___ ___ ___ ___ on
To school and home again!

I go to school on foot…

7 **Listen again and sing along.**

8 **Play *Yes or No* with a friend.** 💬

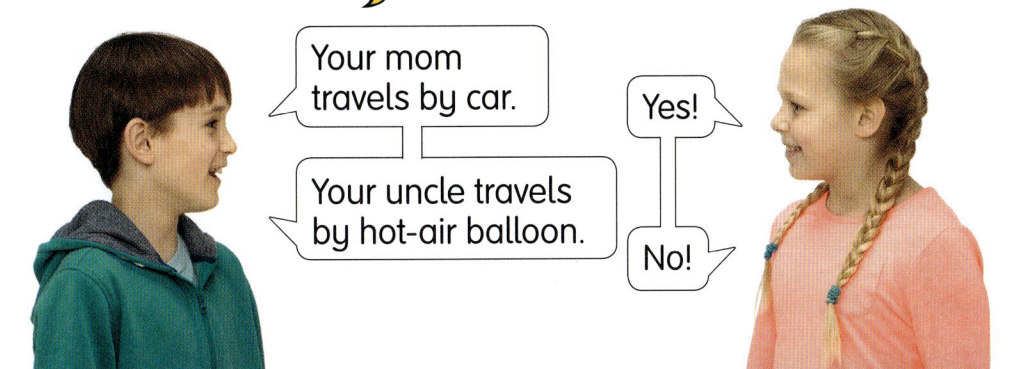

> Your mom travels by car.

> Your uncle travels by hot-air balloon.

> Yes!

> No!

Dad's Tandem

1 **Look at the pictures and discuss with a friend.**

    1 What types of transportation are there in the story?   **2** How do you go to school?

2 **Listen and read along. Write the types of transportation.**

___bus___   _____   _____   _____   _____

1 Billy and his dad are in town. They see a poster on a tree.

Look, Dad! A fair! It's today!

It starts at two o'clock. It's in Bigtown.

2 It's a long way from Billy's house to Bigtown. Billy's dad doesn't have a car.

We can go to the fair on my tandem!

Oh no! Not the tandem!

3 *Sam and his dad are going to the fair by car.*

Look! I can see Sam and his dad!

Are they going by bike?

No, they aren't. That's a tandem. It's for two people.

4 Hannah and her mom are going to the fair by bus.

Look! I can see Hannah and her mom!

Hurry up, Billy! The fair starts at two o'clock!

5 *Theo and his mom are going to the fair by taxi.*

Look! I can see Theo and his mom!

Hurry up, Billy! The fair starts at two o'clock!

6 *Lily and her dad are going to the fair by motorcycle.*

Look! I can see Lily and her dad!

Hurry up, Billy! The fair starts at two o'clock!

7 *A lot of people are going to the fair by car, bus, taxi and motorcycle.* There's a lot of traffic and now there's a traffic jam.

Are they going by tandem?

Yes, they are. They're lucky!

Hurry up, everyone! The fair starts at two o'clock!

8 It's two o'clock. Billy and his dad are at the fair.

WELCOME TO THE FAIR!

Now we can have a lot of time at the fair.

Great! I like traveling by tandem now, Dad!

3 **Act out the story.**

91

1 Look at pages 90–91. Read and mark (✔) the answer.

Are they going by bike?

Yes, they are. ☐

No, they aren't. ☐

Are they going by tandem?

Yes, they are. ☐

No, they aren't. ☐

2 Listen and number. Listen again and check. 🎧 68

Jasmine and her dad ☐

Billy and his dad ☐

Hannah and her mom ☐

Suzy and her dad ☐

Jenny and her grandma ☐ 1

Nick and his grandma ☐

Jessie and her dad ☐

Jack and his mom ☐

3 Read and complete the answers.

1 Are Jasmine and her dad going to the fair by bus?   Yes, _they are_____ .

2 Are Suzy and her dad going to the fair by car?   Yes, _____ .

3 Are Billy and his dad going to the fair on foot?   No, _____ .

4 Are Nick and his grandma going to the fair by motorcycle?   _____ .

5 Are Jessie and her dad going to the fair on foot?   _____ .

4 Look at the picture in Activity 2 and complete the questions.

1 Are Jenny and her grandma going to the fair __by bus__? No, they aren't.

2 _____ Jessie and her dad _____ to the fair _____ foot? Yes, they are.

3 _____ Jack and his mom _____ to the fair _____? Yes, they are.

4 _____ Suzy and her dad _____? No, they aren't.

5 Look at the pictures. Write questions and answers.

1 (helicopter) _Are they going by helicopter?_
No, they aren't. They're going by plane.

2 (bike) _____
_____

3 (train) _____
_____

4 (bus) _____
_____

6 Cover the text in Activity 5. Play *Find the Picture* with a friend.

Are they wearing jackets?

Are they going by bike?

Yes, they are.

No, they aren't.

June's Tune

1 **Match the word with the pictures. Listen and check.** 🎧 69

- ☐ bridge
- ☐ country
- ☐ left
- ☐ path
- ☐ right
- ☐ river
- 1 street
- ☐ town

2 **Read and complete with words from Activity 1. Listen and check.** 🎵 70

Riding along on a tandem
Two big wheels and four feet, too.
Riding along on a tandem
Two big wheels and four feet, too.

Can you tell me the way to the fair?
Go along the **(1)** ___street___ . It's over there!
Turn **(2)** _____ and **(3)** _____ .
Go up and down,
From the **(4)** _____ to the **(5)** _____ .

Riding along …

Can you tell me the way to the fair?
Go along the **(6)** _____ !
The **(7)** _____ is there!
Go across the **(8)** _____ . Go up and down,
From the country to the town.

Riding along …

3 **Listen again and sing along.**

4 **Read and complete the directions.**

Can you tell me the way to the fair?

(1) ___Go along___ the street.
(2) _____ left and right.
(3) _____ the bridge.
(4) _____ the country to the town.

Grammar

Can you tell me the way to the	school? zoo?

Grammar

	along	the path / the street / the river.		
Go Ride	across	the bridge.		
	from	the town / country	to	the town / country.
Turn	left / right.			

5 **Look at the map and complete the questions and answers.**

café   hospital   lake   ~~park~~

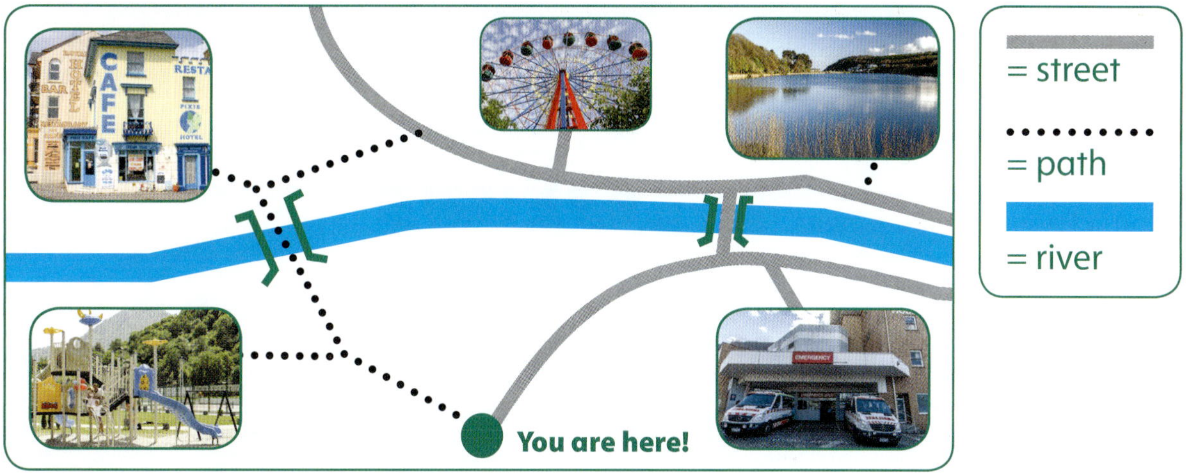

= street
········· = path
= river

You are here!

1
Can you tell me the way to the ___park___?

2
Can you tell me the way _____?

3
Can you tell me _____ ?

4
_____
_____
fair?

Go along the path and turn left.

Go along the street and turn right.

Go along the path and across the bridge. Turn left.

Go _____ the street. Turn _____ and go across the _____ over the _____. Turn _____, then turn _____ and go along the _____.

6 **Work with a friend. Find a different route to the fair. Write the directions.**

7 **Complete your map and play.** **W B** **125**

Can you tell me the way to the zoo?

Go along the street. Turn left. Go along the street and along the path.

Rose Knows about ...

Bicycle Safety

1 Read and circle the words. Listen and check. 🎧 71

Riding a bike is fun, but it is important to be safe, too. Follow these important rules:

1 Use the correct **people** / **equipment**

Use a light to help people see you at night. Also, use a *bell* to tell people you are there. Use a *backpack* to carry things safely and wear a *helmet* to protect your head.

2 Wear the correct **clothes** / **places**.

Wear *bright clothes* to help people see you.

3 Ride in the correct **equipment** / **places**.

Read the *signs* to find out where you can ride. Use quiet roads, *bike lanes* or *bike paths* to stay away from traffic.

4 Respect other **clothes** / **people**.

Be careful when you ride close to other people. Remember to use your bell. And, use a *bike rack* to park your bike safely.

sign

bell

backpack
bright clothes
bike lane or path

light
bike rack

2 Read again and complete the mind map. 📓

2 use lights

3 _____

help people see you?

tell people you are there?

1 _____

4 _____

park your bike safely?

How can you ...

stay away from traffic?

protect your head?

carry things safely?

find out where you can ride?

5 _____

6 _____

7 _____

3 Complete the *Bike Safety Diagram* with words from Activity 2.

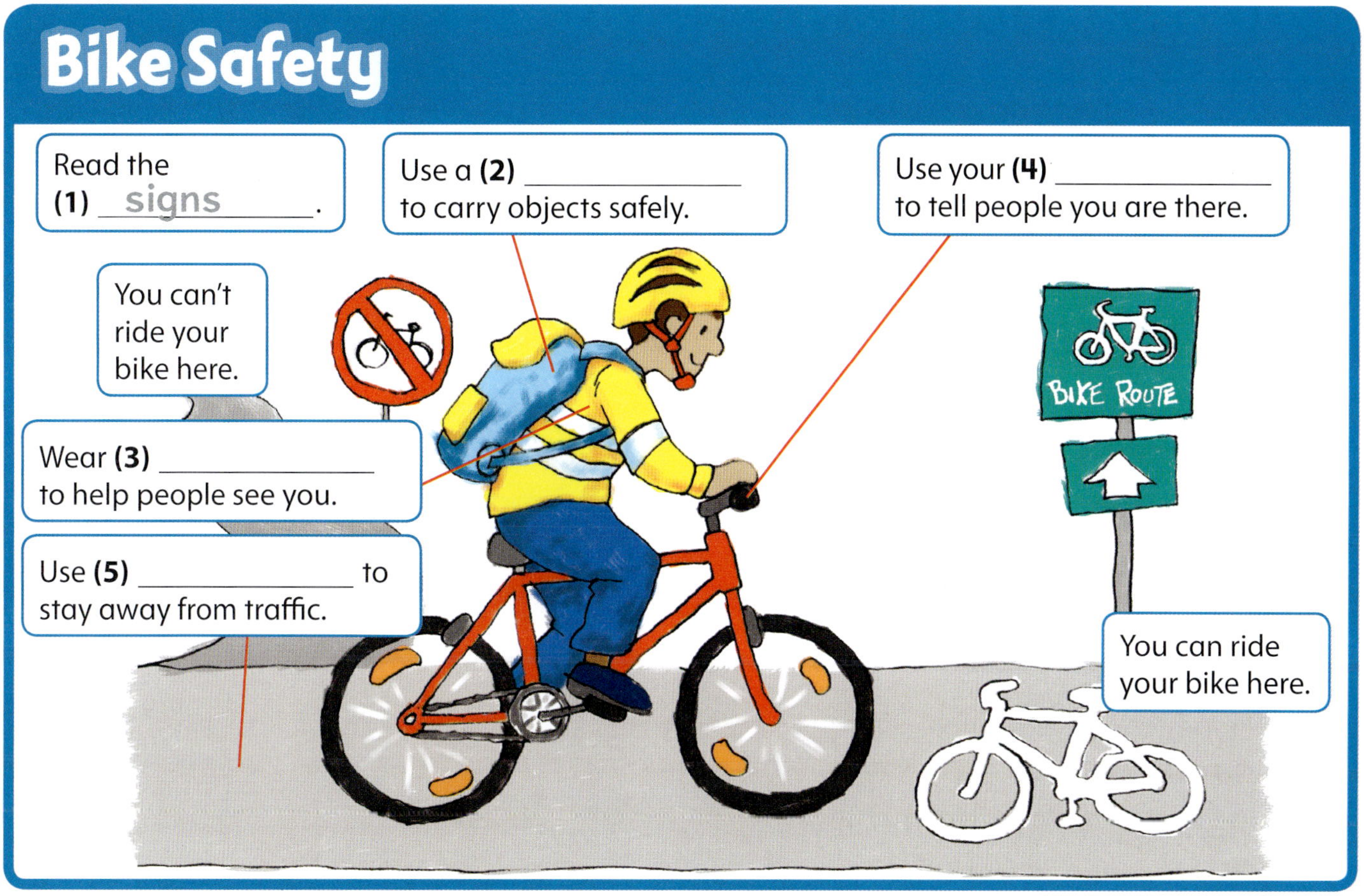

Bike Safety

Read the
(1) __signs__ .

Use a **(2)** _____
to carry objects safely.

Use your **(4)** _____
to tell people you are there.

You can't
ride your
bike here.

Wear **(3)** _____
to help people see you.

Use **(5)** _____ to
stay away from traffic.

BIKE ROUTE

You can ride
your bike here.

4 Create a *Bike Safety Diagram* for your community.

1 Listen and number the pictures.
Listen again and repeat. 🎧 72

2 Listen and repeat the sentences. 🎧 73

A girl is singing to a bird,
wearing a shirt and a skirt.

Claire the fair, sits on a chair in
a hot air balloon, combing her hair.

97

Public Transportation Graph

Jeb's Value ...

Materials

★ Two sheets of grid paper

★ Ruler

★ Pencils and colored pens

⭐ **Read and stick.**

Help reduce pollution.
Use public transportation.

Stage 1: Plan your project.

1. Work in groups. Make a list of all the different transportation that you can use to travel to and from school.

2. Make a chart on grid paper and write the types of transportation.

Stage 2: Develop your project.

1. Get together with your group.
   Ask other group members:
   What type of transportation do you use to travel to and from school? Mark (✔) the different types of transportation on the chart each time.

2. Count the number of marks on the chart. Write the totals.

3. Make a bar graph based on the total results.

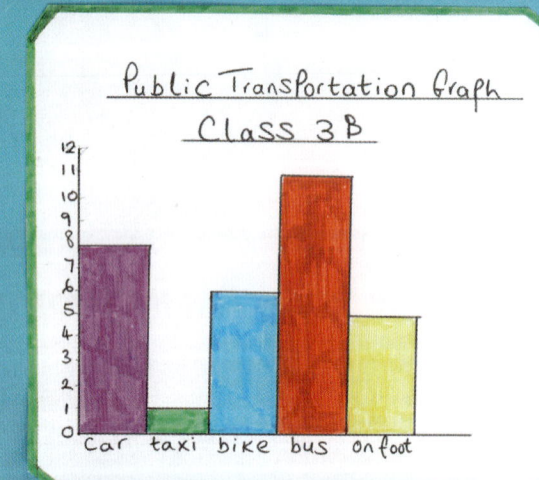

Stage 3: Share your project.

1. Get together with your group. Attach your bar graph to a classroom wall.

2. Walk around the classroom and look at all the bar graphs. Compare and contrast the results of another group with yours.

3. Discuss the similarities or differences with your group. What type of transportation is popular?

Stage 4: Evaluate your project.

Save your *Project Record*.

1 Look and complete the questions and answers.

1 1 Are they going by car ? **3** _____ by bus?

No, they aren't. They are _____ .
going by bike.

2 2 Are _____ **4** _____ by bike?

_____ ? No, _____

Yes, _____ . _____ .

2 Complete the questions and directions.

1 Can you tell me the way to the store?

Go along the path. Turn left. Turn
_____ . Go _____ the bridge
and _____ the street. Turn right.
Turn _____ again.

2 _____ park?

Go along the path. Do not turn right or left.

_____

_____

Park   Zoo

Store

You are here! ➡ ●

3 Write your answers.

What About You?

 What type of transportation do you
use to go to school?

_____

 What do you wear when you ride
your bike?

_____

 Can you tell me the way to school
from your house?

_____

 How do you ride your bike safely?

_____

4 Ask and answer the questions with a friend.

What type of transportation
do you use to go to school?

I go to school on foot.

8 Around Town

Vocabulary

1 Discuss with a friend.

1 What places can you name?

2 Which places are in your town or area?

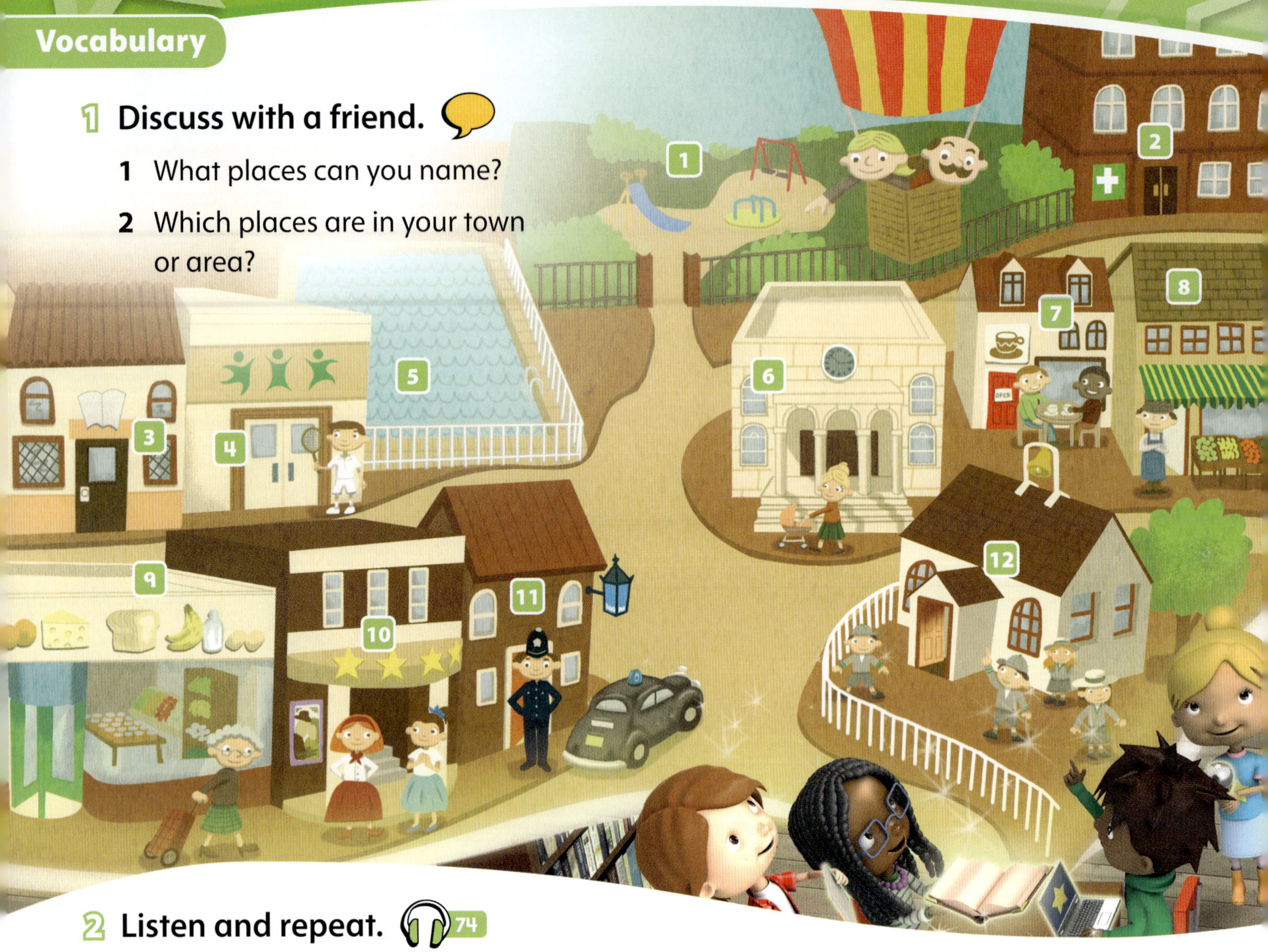

2 Listen and repeat. 74

3 Look and write the words. Listen again and check.

café fitness center grocery store hospital library movie theater
~~park~~ police station school store swimming pool town hall

1 park	4 ________	7 ________	10 ________
2 ________	5 ________	8 ________	11 ________
3 ________	6 ________	9 ________	12 ________

4 Play *Look It Up* with a friend.

Library!

Number three!

5 Read and complete the story.

town

café

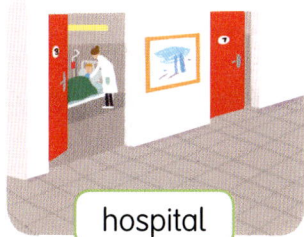
hospital

library

park

school

store

breakfast

Hi, I'm Paul. I live in a big **(1)** ___town___ . My favorite place in town is the
(2) _____ . I go there on Fridays to play with my friends. I like the
(3) _____ , too, because I love books. On Saturdays, I go with my dad to the
(4) _____ to buy fruit and vegetables. On Sundays, Mom, Dad and I go to the
(5) _____ for **(6)** _____ . My mom is a doctor. She works in a
(7) _____ . My dad works at my **(8)** _____ . He's a teacher.

6 Unscramble the words and complete the lyrics. Listen and check. 🎵 75

1 arbiryl   3 icolpe   5 heattre   7 spoiltah

2 sortes   4 ooclsh   6 kpra   8 roryceg

Up in the air in a hot-air balloon,
Up in the air you can see the town,
Up in the air in a hot-air balloon,
Up in the air, up and down.

There's a **(1)** ___library___ , there are
a lot of **(2)** _____ ,
A **(3)** _____ station and a
(4) _____ .
There's a movie **(5)** _____
And a big swimming pool!

Up in the air …

There's a fitness center and a
(6) _____ ,
A café, a town hall.
There's a **(7)** _____
And a big **(8)** _____ store.

Up in the air …

7 Listen again and sing along.

Grandpa's Map

1 Look at the pictures and discuss with a friend. 💬

1 What places can you see in the story?

2 How does the man travel?

2 Listen and read along. Write *true* or *false*. 🎧 76

1 First, Grandpa was in Egypt. ___false___

2 The map was in the café. _____

3 Sara sees the statue in school. _____

4 The treasure is in the garden. _____

1 Sara is at her grandpa's house. He has a lot of mysterious things in his house. One day Sara finds something very mysterious.

What's this, Grandpa?

Ah, yes. It's an old map, but there's a piece missing. It's a mystery.

Tell me the story. *Where were you?*

2 *I was in the library.* It was a long time ago. I was a young man.

What's this? I think it's a map, but there's only one piece! Where are the other pieces? Let's see …

3 It was a map for a hidden treasure. There was a clue on the map.

The 2nd piece of this map is in the café next to DYNEYS Opera House.

Got it! I need to go to Australia. I can go by hot-air balloon.

4 Two months later, *I was in Australia.* The second piece of the map was in the café next to the Sydney Opera House!

There's the café!

The 3rd piece is on a ... in GYPET.

There was another clue. It was easy!

5 Three months later, *I was in Egypt. The third piece of the map was on a pyramid.* There was another clue on the map.

There's the third piece!

The 4th piece is under this.

This clue was very difficult.

6 And that was the story of the map.

I don't know where the statue is. I can't find the treasure. Now I'm old and I can't look for it.

It doesn't matter, Grandpa! *You were in Australia and Egypt!*

The 4th piece is under this.

But the last piece is very important. It shows the treasure!

7 The next day, Sara is in school. She's looking out of the window. Suddenly …

It's the statue!

What?

Everyone, please be quiet!

8 Sara finds the fourth piece of the map! Now Grandpa can find the treasure.

Look! The treasure is in the library garden.

Thank you, Sara!

3 Act out the story.

1 Look at pages 102–103. Match the questions and answers with the picture of the speaker.

1 Where were you?

2 I was in Egypt.

3 I was in the library.

4 You were in Egypt and Australia!

2 Look and complete the answers.

1 Where was Sara at three fifteen?   She was in <u>the swimming pool</u>.

2 Where was Grandpa at six o'clock?   He _____ in the movie theater.

3 Where was Sara at six o'clock?   _____ café.

4 Where was Grandpa at one forty-five?   _____.

3 Unscramble the questions. Match the questions with the answers.

1 at / Sara / o'clock / ? / was / six / Where

   <u>Where was Sara at six o'clock?</u>

   a He was in the grocery store.

2 fifteen / Grandpa / was / Where / at / ? / three

   _____

   b She was in school.

3 forty-five / ? / at / Where / one / Grandpa / was

   _____

   c He was in the park.

4 ? / one / was / Where / at / forty-five / Sara

   _____

   d She was in the café.

4 Listen to the interview and number the pictures.     77

5 Complete the interview questions and answers.

1 Man: Where were you _at eleven fifteen in the morning_____?

Alice: I was in the library with my friends.

2 Man: _____ at seven forty-five in the evening?

Mark: _____ my friend's birthday party.

3 Man: _____ at three thirty in the afternoon?

Anna: I was with my family in _____.

4 Man: _____?

Tony: I was in the kitchen. I have breakfast at eight o'clock.

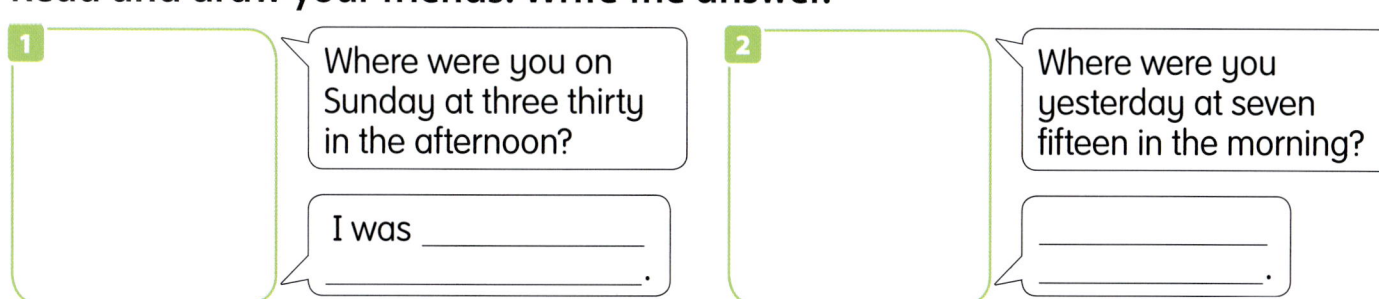

Grammar

Where	was	I / he / she	yesterday?	I / he / she	was	at home.
	were	you / we / they	at two o 'clock?	you / we / they	were	in school.

6 Read and draw your friends. Write the answer.

1

Where were you on Sunday at three thirty in the afternoon?

I was _____ _____.

2

Where were you yesterday at seven fifteen in the morning?

_____ _____.

7 Ask and answer the questions with a friend.

Where were you on Sunday at three thirty in the afternoon?

I was in the park.

June's Tune

1 Look and number the words. Listen and check. 🎵 78

_____ behind the bookstore

__1__ in front of the school

_____ near the swimming pool

_____ opposite the town square

square

bookstore

We're on a trip
In my grandpa's balloon.
Let's find the map!
Let's find it soon!
Where's the map?
It's in front of the school,
Behind the bookstore …
Near the swimming pool!

We're on a trip
In my grandpa's balloon
Let's find the map!
Let's find it soon!
All around town
In my grandpa's balloon,
Let's find it, find it,
find it soon!

We're on a trip
In my grandpa's balloon.
Let's find the map!
Let's find it soon!
Where's the map?
It's opposite the square,
It's not here.
It's over there!

We're on a trip …

2 Listen again and sing along.

Grammar

Where's	the park?	It 's The park is	near opposite behind in front of	the library. the school.

3 Look and complete the answers.

1 Where's the square?
It's opposite __the bookstore__.

2 Where's the school?
It's near _____.

3 Where's the swimming pool?
It's _____.

4 Where's the bookstore?
_____.

4 Look at the map. Complete the questions.

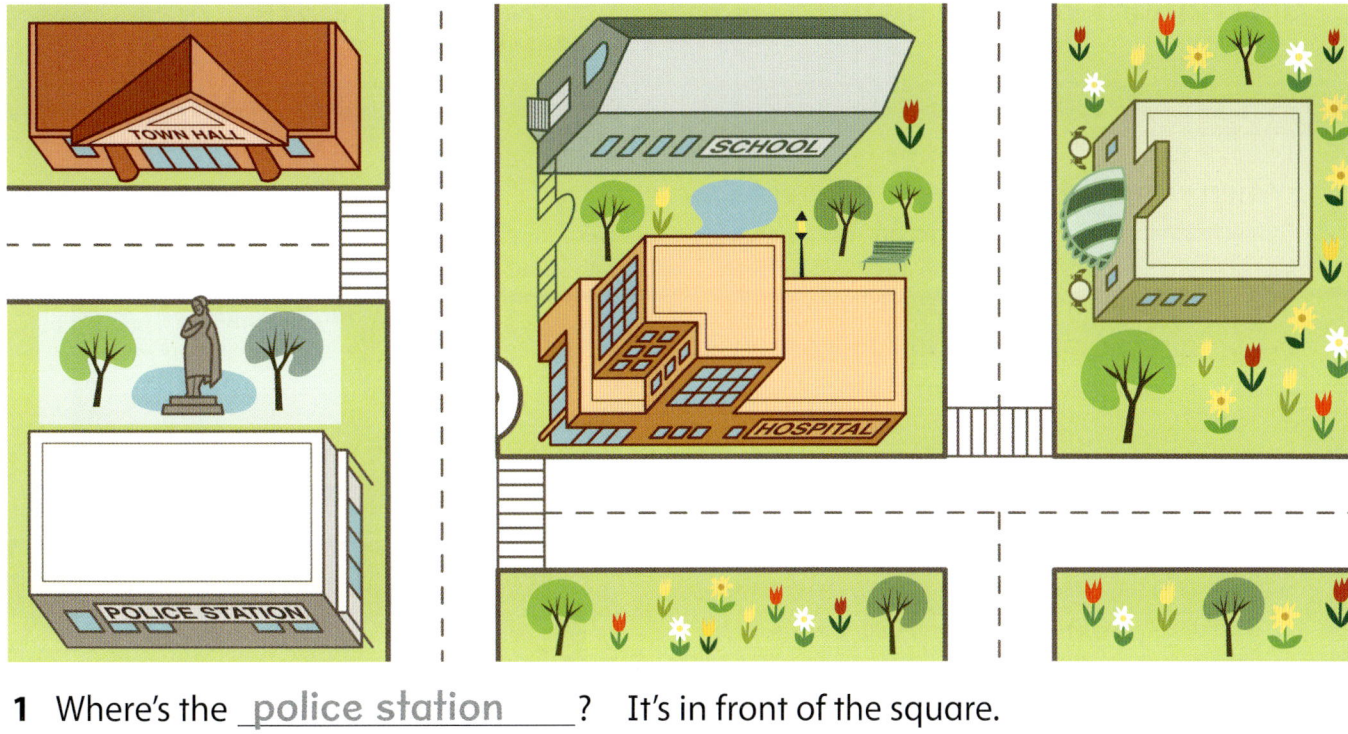

1 Where's the ___police station___ ? It's in front of the square.

2 _____ school? It's opposite the town hall.

3 _____ ? It's near the park.

4 _____ ? It's opposite the hospital.

5 Look at the map again. Write sentences about these places.

1 (school, park)   ___The school is near the park.___

2 (town hall, school)   _____

3 (park, café)   _____

4 (police station, square) _____

6 Write sentences about places where you live. 📝

7 Complete your map and play. W B 126 💬

Where's the bookstore?

It's behind the school.

1 Listen and read along. Match the descriptions with the pictures. 🎧 79

Rose
Knows about ...

Navigation Tools

When we travel, we move in different directions around the earth.

[3] We can use a *compass* to find the direction to travel in. The compass *needle* always points to *north*. The other points on a compass are *south*, *east* and *west*.

[ ] A map usually shows things like roads, mountains, rivers and towns. We can use a map to plan how to go somewhere. We use a compass to help us find north. The compass on the map shows all the different points: *northwest, northeast, southeast* and *southwest*.

[ ] We can use a *Global Positioning System (GPS)* to navigate, too. The GPS uses satellites to tell us where we are and the direction we should go.

The three *navigation tools* can help us find places and travel to different areas without getting lost.

1

2

3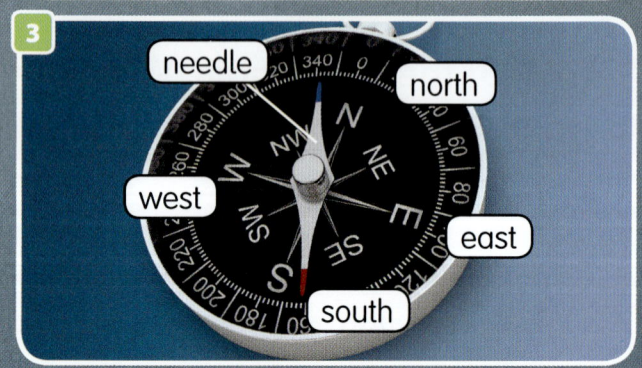

 ## 2 Look at the map in Activity 1 and complete the chart. 📝

To Go from …	To …	You Need to Go …
the forest	the jungle	northwest
the mountains	the desert	
the forest	the beach	
the mountains	the beach	

3 Complete the *Weekend Tour Flyer* with words from Activities 1 and 2.

Castle Fun!

This weekend trip is to the castle. Don't forget to bring your compass or your GPS.

From the start sign, go **(1)** _____east_____ along the path. Walk across the field and go **(2)** _____.

Turn **(3)** _____ and walk past the farmhouse. Go **(4)** _____ and walk past the camping area.

Turn **(5)** _____ and walk on the path to the entrance of the castle.

Enjoy the tour!

4 Write a *Weekend Tour Flyer* for a different place.

1 Listen and number the pictures. Listen again and repeat. 🎧 80

2 Listen and repeat the sentences. 🎧 81

Happy Pam has a rabbit and a bat and a carrot in her bag!

Mark the artist is in the park, painting a starfish and a farmer with dark hair.

Clean Community 3D Map

Materials

* ★ Hand-drawn map
* ★ Glue sticks
* ★ One sheet of cardboard paper
* ★ Pictures of landmarks
* ★ Scissors
* ★ One sheet of poster board
* ★ Large plastic beads

★ **Read and stick.**

Keep your community clean. Don't litter!

Stage 1: Plan your project.

1 Work in groups. Decide which area in your community needs more trash cans.

2 Decide what landmarks you want in your 3D map, like fountains or playgrounds.

Stage 2: Develop your project.

1 Make the map with your group. Glue the map onto the sheet of cardboard paper.

2 Glue the pictures of the landmarks onto the sheet of poster board. Leave a small flap at the bottom of each picture and cut them out. Fold the flaps back. Glue the pictures onto the correct places on the map.

3 Glue plastic beads onto the areas where the new trash cans need to be.

Stage 3: Share your project.

1 Get together with your group. Show your 3D map to other groups.

2 Present your map and explain: How does the location of the trash cans help keep your community clean?

Stage 4: Evaluate your project.  98

Save your *Project Record*.

1 Look and complete the questions and answers.

1 <u>Where was Annie at eight fifteen</u> ?
She was in school.

2 Where _____?
They _____.

3 _____ Tony _____?
_____.

4 Where _____?
They _____.

5 Where's the café?
<u>It's opposite the park</u> .

6 Where's _____?
It's behind the park.

7 _____ the square?
_____.

2 Write your answers.

What About You?

1 Where were you on Saturday afternoon?
_____

2 Where was your mom / dad yesterday morning?
_____

3 Where was your friend at eight fifteen in the morning?
_____

4 Where is your school?
_____

5 What is opposite your house?
_____

6 What is behind your house?
_____

3 Ask and answer the questions with a friend.

Where were you on Saturday afternoon?

I was in the fitness center.

1 Play *Out and About*.

Start   Finish

1 Where's...?

22 ... by train?

21 Can... to the park?

20 Where's...?

19 Where... yesterday... at 4:30?

18 Can... to the hospital?

2 ...by plane?

17 ... by helicopter?

3 Where... yesterday... at 7:45?

= river
= street
= path

police station

swimming pool

movie theater

library

café

grocery store

square

book store

16 Where's...?

4 ... on foot?

fitness center

school

town hall

hospital

park

15 Where... Sunday... at 10:00 o'clock?

5 Can... to the police station?

14 Can... to the fitness center?

6 Where's...?

You are here

13 Where's...?

7 Where.... Friday... at 2:15?

8 Can... to the school?

9 ...by hot-air balloon?

10 Where's...?

11 Can... to the swimming pool?

12 ...by bus?

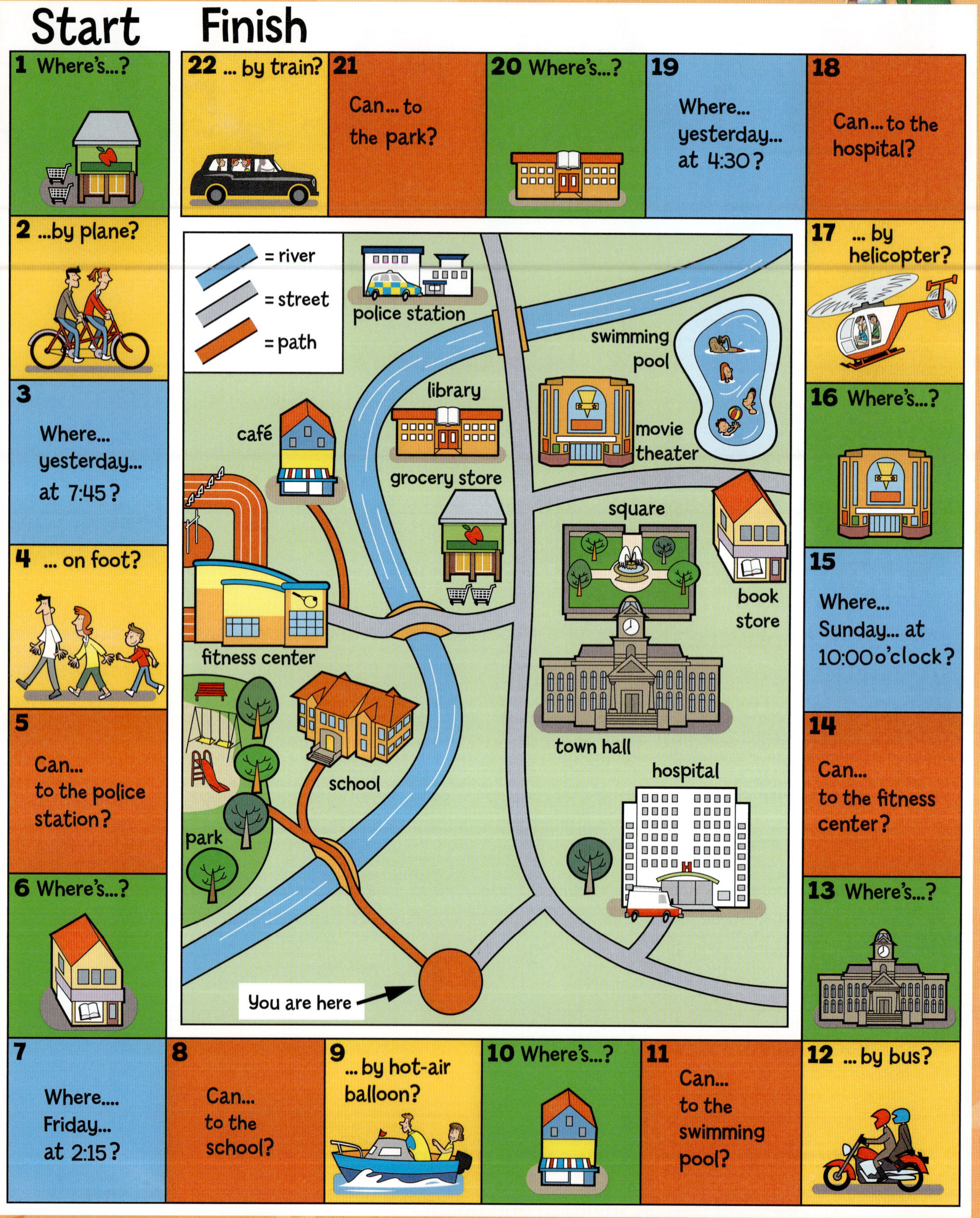

The Netherlands

1 Look at the pictures and circle the objects you can see.

apples   bikes   boats   cheese   (tulips)   water   windmills   wooden shoes

2 Read and number the pictures.

The Netherlands is a small country in Europe. Its capital city is Amsterdam. Most people in the Netherlands speak Dutch. The Netherlands is famous for its delicious cheese. But it is also famous for many other things!

1   Many people travel by boat because there are a lot of canals in the Netherlands. The Dutch also travel by car, bus and train, but a lot of people like traveling by bike. There are a lot of bike paths and bike racks in the towns and in the countryside.

2   Traditional clothes for women include white hats and wooden *clogs*. People wear wooden clogs to keep their feet dry because there is so much water.

3   The countryside has a lot of *tulip* fields. The tulips are of many different colors. The countryside also has many *windmills*. Windmills help pump water from the land.

 3 Complete the chart with the types of transportation.

Types of Transportation	
The Netherlands	Where I live
bike	

9 Summer Camp

1 Discuss with a friend.

1 What objects and places can you name?

2 What objects do you see in the summer?

2 Listen and repeat. 🎧 82

3 Look and number the words. Listen again and check.

___ backpack	___ flashlight	___ lake	___ tent
___ field	___ grass	___ leaves	___ waterfall
___ fire	_1_ hill	___ sleeping bag	___ woods

4 Play *Two in a Row* with a friend. 💬

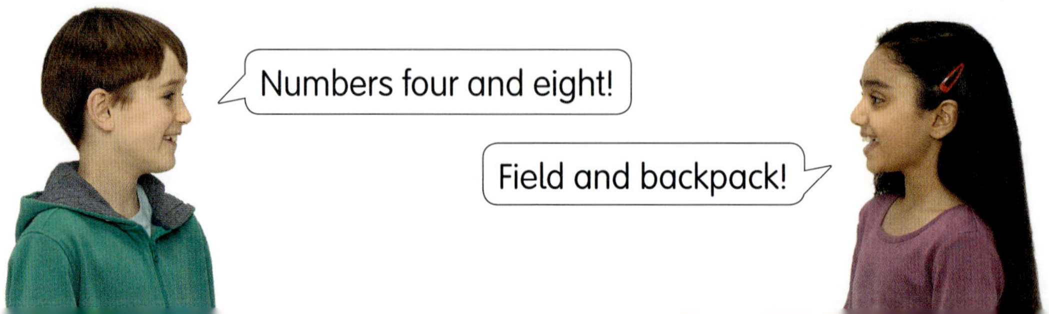

Numbers four and eight!

Field and backpack!

5 Complete the crossword.

Across ▶

Down ▼

1 w a t e r f a l l

6 **Read and complete the words. Listen and check.** 🎵 83

Let's go on a camping trip!
(1) G<u>rass</u> and leaves and a waterfall
Out in the sun on a camping trip!
A hill and a lake! We have it all!

I like running down the **(2)** h_____.
I like walking in the woods
And I like playing in the field.
Camping trips are really good!

Let's go on a camping trip!
Do you have a **(3)** b_____ and
a flashlight?
Around the fire on a camping trip
Do you have a **(4)** s_____ bag?

I like cooking on a fire.
I like fishing on the lake
And I like sleeping in a **(5)** t_____.
Camping trips are really great!

7 Listen again and sing along.

The Missing Sausages

1 **Look at the pictures and discuss with a friend.** 💬

1 How many characters are there in the play?

2 How is the play different from the stories?

2 **Read and complete the play script. Listen and check.** 🎧 84

| cave | dog | ~~fire~~ | flashlight | food | sandwiches | sausages | shoe |

Scene 1: At summer camp

[Pat and friends are next to the fire.]

SAMMY: [HAPPILY] It's the last night of summer camp. What a great party!

PAT: [EXCITEDLY] Oh Sammy, tell us about the party last year!

SAMMY: Ah yes, it was very exciting. Some of the children were next to the ____fire____ with Cook …

Scene 2: Last year's summer camp

[Meg, Jack, Joe, Ollie, Amy and Cook are next to the fire.]

MEG: I'm hungry! What's for dinner?

COOK: Sausages!

JACK: [HAPPILY] They're my favorite _____!

OLLIE: What time is dinner?

COOK: Eight o'clock, and then there's a special concert at nine o'clock.

MEG: [EXCITEDLY] Great!

Scene 3: The missing sausages

SAMMY: [OFFSTAGE] At seven forty-five, it was almost dinnertime and everyone was hungry, but …

COOK: [angrily, looking inside the barbecue] Hey! The _____ are not here!

MEG: [WORRIEDLY] Oh no!

JACK: Where are they?

COOK: I don't know! No sausages, no concert!

Scene 4: Looking for the sausages

SAMMY: [OFFSTAGE] Where were the sausages? *Jack looked around the camp.*

JACK: [POINTING TO THE GROUND] Look! There's a blue earring close to the barbecue!

MEG: It's a clue! [POINTING TO THE GROUND] There are footprints, too.

JOE: [EXCITEDLY] We can follow them to find the sausages.

MEG: [HOLDING UP A FLASHLIGHT] I have a _____.

JOE: [HOLDING UP A COMPASS AND A MAP] I have a compass and a map! Come on!

[Meg turns the flashlight on. Everyone exits.]

SAMMY: [OFFSTAGE] *They walked along the path to the woods.*

Scene 5: At the waterfall

SAMMY: [OFFSTAGE] *The friends climbed the hill and walked to the waterfall.*

[Jack, Meg and Joe enter.]

JOE: [POINTING TO A RED SHOE ON THE GROUND] Look! What's that?

JACK: [PICKING UP THE SHOE] It's a red shoe!

MEG: It's another clue. [POINTING TO THE CAVE] And here's a _____!

[They walk toward the cave.]

Scene 6: Finding the sausages

SAMMY: [OFFSTAGE] Then, there was a noise coming from behind a rock.

[Amy and Ollie appear from behind the rock. They are not happy.]

MEG: It's Amy and Ollie!

JOE: Amy has one blue earring!

MEG: Ollie has one red _____!

JACK: And they have the sausages!

[Amy and Ollie hold up the sausages.]

Scene 7: The little dog

SAMMY: [OFFSTAGE] Then *a little dog jumped out of the cave.*

[A little dog jumps out of the cave.]

OLLIE: [WORRIEDLY] The sausages were for the _____. It was hungry.

AMY: It's a very friendly little dog.

Scene 8: Back at the camp

SAMMY: [OFFSTAGE] *The friends walked back to the camp with the little dog.*

[Joe, Jack, Meg, Ollie and Amy enter.]

JACK: It's almost time for the concert and there's no dinner.

COOK: Amy and Ollie can help me make some _____.

OLLIE: Yes, OK. Sorry everyone!

3 Act out the play.

1 Order Sammy's story (1–5). Look at pages 116–117 and check.

[ ] They climbed the hill and walked to the waterfall.

[ ] A little dog jumped out of the cave.

[ ] They walked along the path to the woods.

[ ] The friends walked back to the camp with the little dog.

[1] Jack looked around the camp.

2 Look and complete the answers.

cooked   ~~fished~~   played   walked

1 What did Joe do yesterday afternoon?

He ___fished___ on the lake.

2 What did Amy do yesterday afternoon?

She _____ on a fire.

3 What did Sammy do yesterday afternoon?

He _____ to the waterfall.

4 What did Meg do yesterday afternoon?

She _____ with Sammy.

3 Match the pictures with the questions and answers. Complete the questions.

 [ ]    [1]    [ ]    [ ]

1 What _____did_____ Jack do yesterday? He painted a picture.

2 _____ Jack do last Sunday? He jumped across the river.

3 _____ Meg _____ last week? She climbed a hill.

4 _____ Sammy _____ yesterday? He looked around the park.

4 **Listen and match the day with the picture.**  85

Monday

Tuesday

Wednesday

Thursday

Friday

Saturday

Sunday

Grammar

What	did	I you he / she / it we they	do	yesterday? last week? last night?	I You He / She / It We They	climbed the hill / tree. looked around the camp. jumped across the river. walked to the waterfall. cooked / fished / painted / played.

5 **Look at the pictures in Activity 4 and complete the sentences.**

1 On Monday, Daisy _walked up a hill_____.

2 On Tuesday, she _____.

3 On Wednesday, _____.

4 On _____.

6 **Write sentences about your week.**

7 **Play *What Did You Do?* with a friend.**

What did you do yesterday?

I played basketball with my friends.

119

June's Tune

1 **Complete the instructions with a friend. Listen and check.** 🎧 86

| close | litter | pick | protect | ~~put out~~ | walk |

1 _Put out_ fires.

4 _____ on the paths.

2 Don't _____.

5 Don't _____ the flowers.

3 _____ the animals.

6 _____ the gates.

2 **Listen and sing along.** 🎵 87

We're in the country on holiday!
We're in the country, it's a sunny day!
Walk in the woods! Come on, let's go!
But don't forget the country code!

Don't drop litter here and there!
Don't pick flowers anywhere!

We're in the country …

Walk on the path through fields and woods!
Close the gate! That's very good!

We're in the country …

Protect the animals, everyone!
And put out the fire! Good! Well done!

We're in the country …

3 **Match to complete the instructions.**

1 Close	fires.	animals.
2 Protect	the	
3 Don't	pick	flowers.
4 Put out	litter.	gates.

Grammar

Protect	the animals.	
Turn	right.	
Don't	ride	your bike here.
	pick	the flowers.

4 **Complete your picture and play.** 📖127 💬

Don't litter. B2?

No, my turn. Don't litter. A1?

Yes! Your turn, again.

5 Read the text. Choose the right words and write them on the lines.

1 Do you like ___walking___ in the countryside? It is important to protect the countryside and follow

2 the code. Walk _____ the paths, and close the gates.

3 _____ litter. Put your garbage in a trash can! You can take photos, but

4 don't _____ the flowers. There

5 _____ a lot of animals in the fields and in the woods.

6 _____ the animals and don't feed them!

1	walks	(walking)	walked
2	in	to	on
3	And	Don't	Here
4	pick	picked	picking
5	is	a	are
6	protecting	Protect	protected

6 Look at the signs and complete the instructions.

feed   put   ride   turn   ~~walk~~   wear

a helmet   your horse   left   ~~on the grass~~   the birds   your garbage

1 Don't _walk_ _on the grass_ .

3 Don't _____ _____ here.

5 Don't _____ _____ .

2 _____ _____ in the trash can.

4 _____ _____ .

6 _____ _____ here.

1 Listen and read along.
Write the numbers. 🎧 88

Rose Knows about ...

The Water Cycle

Water is present in nature in three different states: *solid*, *liquid* and *gas*.

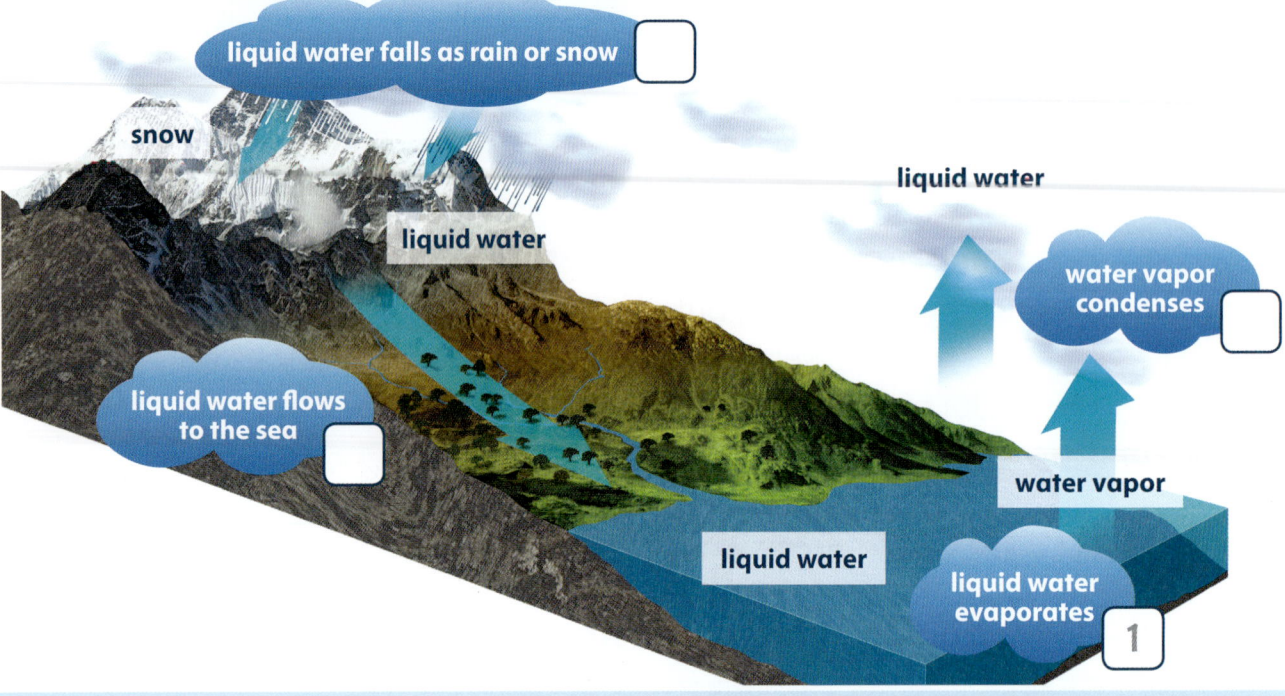

liquid water falls as rain or snow

snow

liquid water

liquid water

water vapor condenses

liquid water flows to the sea

water vapor

liquid water

liquid water evaporates **1**

① On warm days, liquid water *evaporates*—it changes to *water vapor* or a *gas*. It goes up into the air.

② In the air, the water vapor gets colder and *condenses*—it changes to a liquid. The liquid water forms *droplets*, and the droplets form clouds. We cannot see water vapor until it starts to *condense* in the air.

③ When there are a lot of droplets in the sky, the liquid water falls as rain. When it is very cold, the water *freezes*—it changes to a solid, like ice or snow, and it falls.

④ Snow *melts*—it changes to liquid water. The liquid water in rivers flows to the sea.

2 Read again and complete the flow chart.

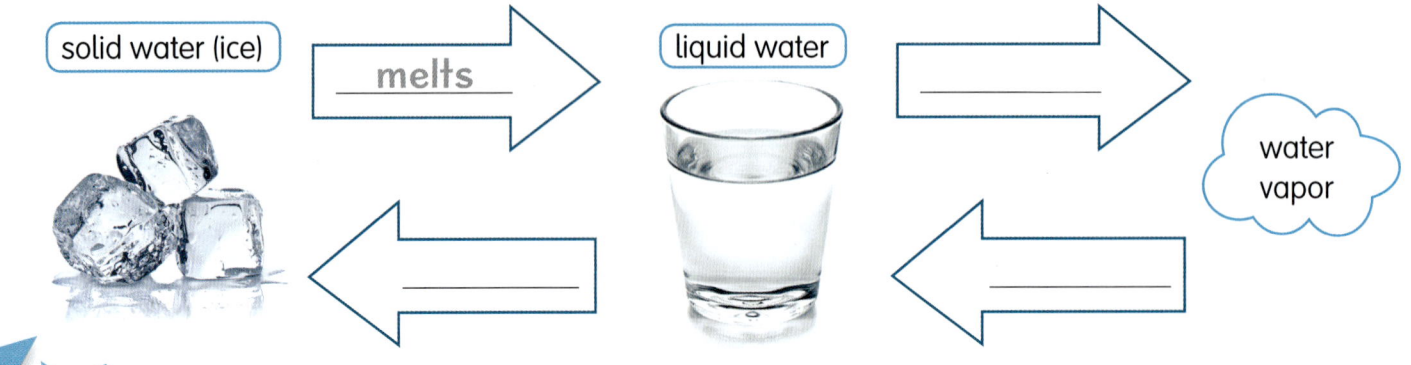

solid water (ice) → _melts_ → liquid water → _____ → water vapor

_____ ← _____ ←

3 Complete the *Water Use Poster* with words from Activities 1 and 2.

Water in my life

I use **(1)** ____solid____ water when …

I go ice skating.

I use **(2)** _____ water when …

I wash the car.

I take a shower.

I use **(3)** water _____ when …

I iron my shirt.

Liquid water **(4)** _____ when …

I put it in the freezer.

Ice **(5)** _____ when …

I put it in a drink.

Some liquid water **(6)** _____ when …

I take a bath.

Water vapor **(7)** _____ when …

the windows are cold.

4 Make a *Water Use Poster* with your own examples.

1 Listen and number the pictures. Listen again and repeat. 🎧 89

2 Listen and repeat the sentences. 🎧 90

Hi Bill!

I jump**ed** around and cook**ed** my dinner.
I fish**ed** in the river, then walk**ed** to town!

They clos**ed** the gate and climb**ed** a hill.
They call**ed** Bill and then play**ed** a game!

Water Fact Poster

Jeb's Value ...

Materials

★ One sheet of poster board

★ Ruler and pencil

★ Colored pens and pencils

★ **Read and stick.**

Save water when you can.

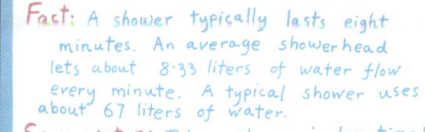

Fast: A shower typically lasts eight minutes. An average showerhead lets about 8.33 liters of water flow every minute. A typical shower uses about 67 liters of water.

Save water: Take a shower in less time!

Stage 1: Plan your project.

1 Work in groups. Make a list of the ways in which people use water.

2 Think of categories. Write your ideas on a chart.

3 Find out how much water people use in daily activities, for example: taking a shower or using a dishwasher. Choose one daily activity and think about how to save water.

Stage 2: Develop your project.

1 Get together with your group. Divide the poster board sheet into two parts.

2 On the left of the poster board sheet, draw the daily activity you chose.

3 On the right of the poster board sheet, write the facts and your ideas on how to save water.

Stage 3: Share your project.

1 Get together with your group. Attach your poster to a classroom wall.

2 Walk around the classroom and look at all the posters.

3 Discuss with your group. Which ideas help save water?

Stage 4: Evaluate your project.

Save your *Project Record*.

1 Look and complete the questions and answers. Complete the rules.

1 What did she do _____ last weekend?

_____ .

2 _____ ?

He painted a picture.

3 _____ ?

They _____ .

4 (ride, bike) Don't ride _____ your bike here.

5 (walk, path) _____ on _____ .

6 (litter) _____ !

2 Write your answers.

What About You?

 What did you do yesterday?

_____

 What did you do last weekend?

_____

 What did you do last night?

_____

 What did your friends do last weekend?

_____

 What rules do you have in school?

_____

 How do you use liquid water at home?

_____

3 Ask and answer the questions with a friend.

| What did you do yesterday? | I walked in the park. |

The School Show

1 **Look at the pictures and discuss with a friend.**

    1 How many characters are there in the story?   **2** What places can you name?

2 **Listen and circle the words. Listen and check.** 91

1 It's Saturday, July 20th. It's almost three **fifteen** / **thirty**. The students are in the school auditorium.

We're ready!

The costumes and scenery look great!

I'm so excited!

Me, too!

2 But the school auditorium is empty. There aren't any people! The students and Miss Snow are very worried.

Where's everyone?

Where are our friends?

Maybe they don't know about the show.

That's impossible! There are a lot of posters!

3 Last week, the students were in the **country** / **town** with the posters.

I walked to the café **along** / **opposite** the movie theater. There's a poster in the café. There are two posters in the bookstore next to the café.

4 June rode her bike across the **bridge** / **café** and along the river to the town.

There's a poster in the grocery store and there's a poster in the library between the police station and the fitness center.

5 Rory walked to the town hall.

There are two **students / posters** in the town hall and there are three posters in the park behind the town hall.

SHOW!
3:15 pm to 4:15 pm

SHOW! Saturday, 30th July

And there's the website, too!

6 Suddenly, the students and Miss Snow hear a noise.

What's that?

I don't know.

It's coming from outside.

Let's go look!

7 There are a lot of people outside, but the door is locked.

Look! Here's everyone!

We can't come in!

Oops!

Quick! Here's the **book / key**!

8 Now there are a lot of people in the school auditorium. The show can begin.

… Tell us about the party last year.

Ah yes …

This **student / show** is great!

Yes! They're very smart students!

3 **Act out the story.**

Syllabus	Vocabulary	Structures	Phonics	Cross-Curricular Themes	Cultural Values
S	Classroom objects Ordinal numbers 1st – 31st	When's your birthday? It's on April 25th. What's your phone number / name / last name? Whose is this? Pronouns			
1	Descriptions Adjectives to Describe People	Does he / she have (glasses)? Yes, he / she has. He's / She's clever, but he's / she's grumpy.	sand vs. stands Revision: juice	Art: Portraits	Be quiet and listen when other people are performing
2	Sports (-ing forms) Sports Verbs	Does he / she like (swimming)? Yes, he / she does. / No, he / she doesn't. What's he / she doing? He/She's (throw)ing the ball.	chicken vs. sheep Revision: house	P.E.: Safe Sports	Exercise every day
3	Jobs A Doctor's Equipment	Can the aliens / they (speak English)? Yes, they can. / No, they can't. Can he / she (use a computer)? Yes, they can. / No, they can't. Whose is / are (this bandage / these plasters)? They're Dr Zig's / his.	teeth vs. old Revision: water	Science: Astronauts	Protect your clothes. keep them neat
4	Zoo Animals Habitats	Is it (running)? Yes, it is. / No, it isn't. Do they / hippos live (in water)? Yes, they do. / No, they don't.	earring vs. melon Revision: teacher	Science: Animal Habitats	Protect the habitat of animals in your area
5	Food Meal Times and Prepositions of Time	Would you like (a burger / some toast)? Yes, please. / No, thank you. I have (breakfast) in the morning. I have (toast) for (breakfast).	pig vs. beach Revision: drum	Science: Healthy Eating	Eat healthy food to get the nutrients you need
6	Daily Routine Telling the Time	He/She (wakes up), he / she (gets up) and then (has a shower). What time does he / she (get up)? He / she gets up at (seven forty-five).	phone vs. frog Revision: rabbit	Math: Time Zones	Complete your assignments on time
7	Transportation Directions and Places Related to Transportation	Are they going by (bus?) Yes, they are. / No, they aren't. Can you tell me the way to (the zoo)? Go up / down / along / across. Turn left / right.	girl vs. fair Revision: teeth	P.E.: Bicycle Safety	Help reduce pollution. Use public transportation
8	Places in the Town Directions	Where were you? I was in the (movie theater). You were in the (park) The (grocery store) is in front of the (café).	happy vs. park Revision: football	Geography: Navigation Tools	Keep your community clean. Don't litter!
9	Camping Places and Equipment Country Code	I/You/He/She/We (walk)ed to the waterfall. Don't litter! Walk on the path!	fished /t/ vs. climbed /d/ Revision: photo	Science: The Water Cycle	Save water when you can